Due Return Date Date	Due Return Date Date

PROGRESSIVE AND
CONSERVATIVE MAN

DUQUESNE STUDIES
Philosophical Series

27

PROGRESSIVE AND CONSERVATIVE MAN

by

Herman H. Berger

Duquesne University Press, Pittsburgh, Pa.
Editions E. Nauwelaerts, Louvain

DUQUESNE STUDIES
PHILOSOPHICAL SERIES

Titles in Print

Andrew G. van Melsen and Henry J. Koren, editors.

Volume Six—*P. Henry van Laer*, THE PHILOSOPHY OF SCIENCE. Part One: Science in General. Pp. XVII and 164. Second edition. Price: cloth $3.75.

Volume Eight—*Albert Dondeyne*, CONTEMPORARY EUROPEAN THOUGHT AND CHRISTIAN FAITH. Pp. XI and 211. Third impression. Price $5.75. Published also in French.

Volume Nine—*Maxwell J. Charlesworth*, PHILOSOPHY AND LINGUISTIC ANALYSIS. Pp. XIII and 234. Second impression. Price: paper $4.75, cloth $5.50.

Volume Eleven—*Remy C. Kwant*, ENCOUNTER. Pp. VIII and 85. Second impression. Price: cloth, $3.25. Published also in Dutch.

Volume Twelve—*William A. Luijpen*, EXISTENTIAL PHENOMENOLOGY. Pp. 409. Revised Edition. Price: cloth $8.95. Published also in Dutch and Spanish. German edition in preparation.

Volume Thirteen—*Andrew G. van Melsen*, SCIENCE AND TECHNOLOGY. Pp. X and 273. Price: paper $6.20, cloth $6.95. Published also in Dutch and German. Polish edition in preparation.

Volume Sixteen—*John A. Peters*, METAPHYSICS: A SYSTEMATIC SURVEY. Pp. XVIII and 529. Price: paper $9.00, cloth $9.75. Published also in Dutch.

Volume Seventeen—*William A. Luijpen*, PHENOMENOLOGY AND ATHEISM. Pp. XIV and 342. Second impression. Price: $4.25. Published also in Dutch.

Original Dutch language edition, De Progressieve En De Conservatieve Mens, published by Dekker & van de Vegt, Nijmegen, Holland.
Copyright © 1969 by Dekker & van de Vegt

First Printing

Library of Congress catalog card number: 70-125032

Standard Book Number: 8207-0132-7

PRINTED IN THE UNITED STATES OF AMERICA

CONTENTS

PREFACE

This book has been translated directly from the original Dutch text by the undersigned. The author has personally read and approved the translation. The text deviates from the original only in a few minor points. The indexes have been added by the translator for the convenience of the readers.

We wish to express our thanks to Dr. James Erpenbeck for suggesting some corrections and improving the readability of the work.

Henry J. Koren

INTRODUCTION

Contemporary theology is confronted with the question as to what exactly belongs to the authentic faith of the Church. As Cardinal Alfrink of Holland has pointed out in a recent address, it is precisely this question which in the contemporary community of believers constitutes the cause of great uncertainty, restlessness and anxiety. He therefore asked: "Isn't it possible to find a way to bridge the opposition at least to a certain extent," isn't it possible to make the Catholic community return to an attitude of "tolerance, mutual understanding and authentic dialogue?"[1]

These present-day oppositions obviously are not a typically Dutch phenomenon but manifest themselves throughout the whole Church; they are not even limited to the Catholic Church but occur also in other Christian communities. This means that they cannot be exclusively a consequence of Catholic theology. The present evolution in the Christian theologies is the repercussion of a prior development that occurred in all realms of life and that, as usual, found expression in philosophy earlier than in theology. This is the reason why a good understanding of the theological development demands familiarity with the philosophical evolution.

This book attempts to sketch the philosophical evolution by concentrating on a few topics which play an important role in contemporary thought. In all of them the focal point lies in the opposition between the progressive and the conservative man. The

---

[1] *Katholiek Archief*, 1968, vol. 23, no. 24, col. 1079-1083.

author makes no attempt to conceal his option in favor of progressivity, but does not at all have the intention to intensify the opposition. On the contrary, as will gradually become evident, that opposition—progressive-conservative—is incomplete. Ultimately there are three human attitudes which play a role here, viz., progressivity, conservatism and rebellion. This idea, we think, should be able to soften the contrast between progressive and conservative. Being progressive is essentially different from rebellion; one can only be progressive on the basis of great attention to the past. What the progressive man wants is precisely to preserve the truth of the past in the only way truth can be preserved.

CHAPTER ONE

Three Views Of Philosophy

European philosophy has a long history, in which it did not always understand itself in the same way. We will present here a sketch of its development. But this chapter does not have a purely informative function. For by ascribing value to this development, we also present a first description of the standpoint from which the subsequent considerations should be viewed.

1. Philosophy as "Theoria"

Thales of Miletus can serve as an appropriate symbol of Greek philosophy, particularly on the basis of two anecdotes. He taught, so Aristotle relates, that water is the primary stuff of all things and that all things are full of gods, but these assertions hardly suffice to bring him out in full relief. More eloquent is the story that he could have become rich if he had wished. He proved this on one occasion, when he foresaw that there was going to be an excellent harvest of olives and cornered the market in oil by renting all oil-presses.[1] Yet he did not die a rich man, for he was not interested in money. His interests lay in a different direction, one that made him a symbol even for Plato. The latter relates that Thales fell into a well as he was looking up at the stars, so that his maid laughed at him: "You are so eager to know the heavens that you cannot see what lies before your feet" (*Theaetetus*, 174 ab). And Plato adds that

---

[1] Diogenes Laërtius, *Lives and Opinions of Eminent Philosophers*, I, 22-44 (Loeb Classical Library).

this jest is applicable to all philosophers: they become ridiculous when they try to move around in the world as other people do.

Strictly speaking, Socrates offers the same picture. True, Socrates was a city-dweller who rarely left Athens because, he said, trees and flowers could not teach him anything; yet he was not an ordinary citizen. Although he may have learned a trade, he did not practice it. When he was brought to trial for having introduced new gods and corrupting the young and it became evident that his prospects for acquittal were very dim, a proposal was made which would have saved both him and the city of Athens from a condemnation: he would be set free on condition that he would no longer try to involve all kinds of people in the dialogues he was accustomed to have with them. But Socrates rejected this proposal, saying that he could not allow himself to cease being a philosopher.

What was that philosophy that was going to cost him his life? To speak with people, to admonish then, to tell them that it is wrong to worry about money, honor and glory, but not about the truth, not about the soul. Was the Greek philosopher, then, a moralist? No, something else is involved, viz., the opposition between money and honor on the one hand and truth and soul on the other. The philosopher's love is different from that of the non-philosopher. In daily life people worry about money and glory, but the philosopher does not feel at home in the world of daily life. One whose life is encompassed by daily life has no time for philosophy. The fact that people have no time arises from man's bodily being. The body requires much work, for it wants to be fed, it is subject to diseases, and fills us with desires. The desire for money and glory causes fights and wars. Thus the bodily man has no time for truth. This is the reason why philosophers break contact with the everyday world.

Because they have made themselves free for truth, philosophers no longer know how to find the road to the market or the courthouse. They do not take part in festivities and are ignorant of the slanderous tales others indulge in. Only their bodies dwell in the city; with their thoughts they are everywhere at once. Thales is the prototype of the philosopher. The philosopher is the only one who has grown up in authentic freedom. For the man of the world never has time; he is a slave of Necessity. In its service he learns to

speak clever and flattering words. But his soul becomes small and
distorted because it is deprived of free growth by the slavery with
which it has been afflicted since youth. At the end there remains
nothing healthy in his thinking. That's why he rejects philosophy.
Philosophy, he says, is an interesting pursuit for the young. The
stuttering of a child can sometimes be charming; one who is still a
child can busy himself with philosophy. But an adult who still
stutters or philosophizes deserves a sound thrashing, for he ought to
be at home in the world, the world which the philosopher flees
from. To this the philosopher replies that he flees from the daily
world only for the sake of a higher life: "To fly away means to
become like God, as far as this is possible" for man (*Theaetetus*,
176b).[2]

This leads us to the Greek view of philosophy. Philosophy demands freedom from worry about the necessities of life in order to
be free for discourse. Philosophy sprang from the lineage of the
crickets, which, as a special gift of the Muses, require no nourishment once they are born and can keep singing, without eating and
drinking, until they die (*Phaedrus*, 258e-259e). That's why the
discourse of philosophers cannot be concerned with the petty news
of everyday, of who has married and who has become what. Their
discourse has no other topic than what Socrates called truth and
the soul. The purpose of their discourse is *theoria*.

This portrait of the philosopher is strongly influenced by Plato.
But Aristotle, too, remained faithful to the ideal of *theoria*, contemplation. He also knew various types of life. Money, he says, cannot
be the highest end of life, for money is a means. A life devoted to
pleasure is suitable to beasts. People of superior refinement prefer
political life, the end of which is honor. But honor depends on
other people, while what we are looking for is something proper to
a man and not easily taken away from him. Besides, the object of
political life is our fellowman, but man is not the highest being in
the world. Celestial bodies, for example, are obviously much more
divine than is man. Contemplative life, on the other hand, is based
on what is most divine in man and aims at what is most divine in

---

2 Cf. Herman Berger, "Vrije tijd en gesprek volgens Plato," *Roeping*, Juli-
Augustus, 1958, pp. 155-171.

the cosmos. That's why only contemplative life can make us really happy, and why contemplation is the activity which man can exercise most continuously.

Moreover, one cannot be just unless there is a fellowman with respect to whom he practices this virtue. The philosopher, on the other hand, does not need his fellowman in order to be able to philosophize. Again, contemplation shows its excellence by the fact that it is not useful but is pursued for its own sake. And while the politician is always busy, the philosopher is genuinely at leisure. Man would be supremely happy, therefore, if he could devote himself exclusively to contemplation. But such a life would be beyond his power; it is the privilege of the gods. Man is capable of contemplation only to the extent that he has a divine element within himself. For this reason his happiness remains incomplete.[3]

Similar considerations are found in Augustine and Thomas Aquinas. Book III of the latter's *Contra gentes* actually is a broad development of the above-mentioned ideas. *Theoria* remained the ideal of the Christian Middle Ages, which called it contemplation or contemplative life. The Christian ideal of contemplative life goes back to the Greek presupposition that one must withdraw from everyday life, even from political life, in order to acquire free time for contemplation.

It stands to reason that in the course of centuries the content of *theoria* or contemplation did not remain unchanged. Philosophy's self-understanding can be seen in the gradual disappearance and change of such content. In the present case we must say that the active implications of the Greek term *theoria* became weaker in the Latin translation into *contemplatio*. Both terms, however, are derived from the notion of seeing, a sphere which easily presents itself as an activity in which man is passive. Things present themselves to my seeing. In this way it makes sense to say that our seeing simply finds the things "there." One simply "looks on." One who knows about wretchedness and need and is simply an observer evidently does not intend to change anything about them; he lets things run their course and does not take action.

---

[3] *Nic. Ethics*, bk. I, ch. 5; bk. VI, ch. 7; bk. X, chs. 7 and 8.

If this attitude constitutes the core of contemplation and if this core became increasingly more evident, one can understand why Plato and Aristotle could be reduced here to the same denominator. Themselves convinced adherents of the contemplative ideal, the medieval philosophers could not yet make this reduction. They followed either Plato or Aristotle, or at least they attempted to reconcile one with the other, thereby showing that in their opinion these two ought to be reconciled. As a matter of fact, Plato starts from an intelligible world, the world of Ideas, while Aristotle begins with the perceptible world, so that the opposition seems to be as great as possible.

As soon, however, as one abandons the ideal of contemplation, it becomes evident that there is more agreement than difference between Plato and Aristotle. The philosopher of contemplation simply finds a world "there." But this world is not at all the everyday world from which he has already withdrawn. It is a higher world. For Plato this higher world is the world of Ideas, for Aristotle it is the essences in perceptible things. Although this difference has its importance, in both cases there is question of a higher world which the philosopher finds already "there." The philosopher remains modest; he readily admits that he will never fully fathom the Ideas or essences. But in this very admission he implies that the higher world is pre-given: it has come from God in an immutable order of higher and lower.

It is obvious that such a philosophy easily becomes the guardian of the established order; it is a stranger to the desire for change. Yet the world must be changed. There is too much injustice in the world, too much superstition, error, misunderstanding, disease. The contrast between the rich and the poor, in particular, becomes increasingly more acute in a world that is more and more industrialized. If philosophy today continues to hold fast to its contemplative character, it degenerates into pure *speculation*. "The philosophers have only *interpreted* the world, in various ways; the point, however, is to *change* it" (Marx[4]).

---

[4] "Theses on Feuerbach," XI, *Selected Works*, Moscow, 1962, vol. 2, p. 405.

2. Unity of Theoria and Praxis

Like Socrates, Karl Marx wished to devote his life to his fellow-men. Socrates' admonished his fellow-citizens to be more concerned about truth and the soul than about honor and money. Marx, on the contrary, thought that people are poor and despised because they are too much concerned about their God and their soul. For religion, he held, is an opiate for the people, an illusory happiness with fatal consequences. Man is poor, wretched, exploited, but he consoles himself with Heaven; he is weak, but considers himself strong because the strong God is his ally. God did not make man, but man made a God for himself. Man epitomized in an imaginary being everything good which all people together in the total course of history are capable of, and this imaginary being man called "God." Man has estranged himself from his own goodness by denying it to himself and then reconstituting it in an imaginary being outside himself. For this reason religion is an alienated form of thinking and an obstacle to man's happiness. Awaiting an illusory happiness, man no longer tries to find his true happiness and resigns himself to his actual misery.

Marx was realistic enough to see that the unhappy man needs his illusions. Thus there is only one thing to do: change the situation in such a way that the need for illusions will automatically disappear. This demands a philosophy that can produce a change. And, first of all, we must realize that the accepted way of philosophizing is an alienation. *Speculation* does not reach reality. A speculative consideration is a false consideration. Only where speculation ceases, does real life begin.

Speculative philosophy, it must be admitted, began only when it withdrew from everyday life, for it was based on the supposition that the everyday world was not the real world. For this reason speculative philosophy resigned itself to the actual defects of the everyday world. It paid attention to the intelligible world, in the conviction that this higher world—as cause, essence and exemplar—would permeate the lower world with its own intelligibility; and so much the worse for the lower world if this had not yet happened to some parts of it. Marx protested that this lower world is the world in which we live and, consequently, the real world, and that the celebrated higher world is an abstraction, a product of thought, of a perverted thinking which wishes to escape from the real world. This flight from reality must be stopped if man is ever to begin his true task. The accepted way of philosophizing must be negated. But it is not easy to negate a philosophy. Nothing is gained by simply turning one's back on it. For if the resigned philosophy is an alienation, it contains a usable core that must be stripped of its alienation. "You cannot transcend philosophy without actualizing it."[5] The estranged philosophy, then, must be criticized.

Again, however, it is not simple to criticize a philosophy. It appears that the critique of a philosophy must start from philosophical presuppositions. But philosophy is estranged; hence the presuppositions share in its alienation. Thus the critique of philosophy seems to become a kind of shadow-show. Yet this is not really the case. A genuine critique of philosophy is possible when one criticizes it from without, in an extra-philosophical way. Such a critique must show that philosophy is not autonomous, not based on independent and eternal truths, as it likes to claim, but itself really belongs to a particular world. That is to say, it belongs to the world of estranged reality which it imagined that it has left behind. It is a mirror reflex of that reality.

The reality in question is estranged because the worker who merely has his power to labor at his disposal, is robbed of the product of his work by the capitalist. The latter disposes of the means of production but himself does not work. As a mirror reflex of this fundamental alienation, philosophy itself also is estranged: unwittingly, it mirrors the established order as the latter is maintained by the capitalistic owners; unwittingly, the ideal of philosophy to withdraw from the everyday course of affairs is dictated by the desire not to be concerned about the real wretchedness of the proletarian. That's why Marx says: "You cannot actualize philosophy without transcending it."

---

[5] "Toward the Critique of Hegel's Philosophy of Law," *Writings of the Young Marx on Philosophy and Society,* ed. by Loyd D. Easton and Kurt H. Guddat, Anchor Books, 1967, p. 256. Cf. "Theses on Feuerbach," II, *Selected Works,* vol. 2, p. 403.

In principle, then, philosophy is actualized, realized, when it breaks its tacit agreement with the capitalist, leaves the established order and acts against its tendency to conservatism. This means that philosophy must abandon the illusion of having eternal truths, which are found to be there already and merely need to be "contemplated." Philosophy must side with the proletarian, for only the proletarian is authentically human. The proletarian is this because he is the only one who works, and being-a-worker and being-human are the same. History is nothing but the process in which man the worker produces himself. Through work nature is transformed, but man is a being-of-nature and, therefore, while working, also produces himself. If the philosopher sides with the proletarian, he opts for productive progress and for the *praxis* of man's becoming-man. This evolving *praxis* does not know any eternal truths. Whether an idea is true or false is something which *praxis* itself must prove or disprove. True philosophy is the unity of *theoria* and *praxis*.

History's development does not run in a straight line but is dialectical. The first task of an authentic philosophy is to discover the course taken by this dialectical development. This philosophy must realize that the proletariat, humiliated and exploited as it still is, is the revolutionary power which holds the future in its hands. For the proletarian possesses nothing but ought to possess everything because he is the one who works and whose labor produces everything. The proletarian is this contradiction, which is the motive power of the dialectical evolution. Authentic philosophy has the task of making the proletarian conscious of his true greatness. This consciousness is an indispensable element of the evolutionary process itself. In this sense it is true that "the proletariat cannot be transcended without the actualization of philosophy."

Obviously, however, philosophy cannot be fully actualized or realized until every alienation is transcended and overcome, the proletarian revolution has occurred and the final communist condition has become a fact. Only then will philosophy realize itself as the unity of *theoria* and *praxis*, no longer in a dialectical but in a

perfect way: "Philosophy cannot be actualized without the transcendence of the proletariat."[6]

Thus far Marx. Let us note that philosophy's self-understanding
did not become immobilized in Marx's way of looking at it. As we
will see later, it is impossible to transcend estrangement totally;
within history the pure definitive condition is not possible. This
means that the perfect unity of *theoria* and *praxis* is impossible
also. Should we then be satisfied with their dialectical unity? That
depends on what exactly one understands by that unity. There is,
however, one fact that should be duly noted, viz., man begins to
work with ideas that precede his work, so that ideas are prior to
work. Marx himself had to admit this. Distinguishing the human
architect from the animal, e.g., from the bee, he says that he
architect preconceives the cell which he wishes to build: "At the
end of every labour-process, we get a result that already existed in
the imagination of the labourer at its commencement."[7]

On the other hand, since Marx philosophy realizes that it is no
longer possible to disregard the so-called lower world. For it is in
this world that the human individuals live and it is there that
history unfolds. This world is real. Man is really a fellowman, and
philosophy is important not only for the solitary spectator but for
the common history of mankind. If the philosopher explores this
world, shedding light on it, and if his explorations give rise to a
"world of essences," of convictions, then the bond uniting these two
worlds is at least just as important as the individual truths he
discovers. Contemplation should not be permitted to be pure
speculation. This is the reason why the relationship between man's
power to theorize and his power to act must be investigated.

3. *Philosophy as Hermeneutics*

Edmund Husserl systematically explored the relationship between the lower and the higher world. He called the everyday

---

[6] *Ibid.*, p. 264.
[7] *Capital*, vol. I, Moscow, 1961, p. 178.

world the "world of the natural attitude" or the "life-world." With a
keen eye for human individuality, he called the one who dwells in
this world not in general "man" but "the natural ego." Next, it is
typical that for Husserl the higher world is twofold: on the one
hand, the world of science, raised by man as the pursuer of
science; on the other, the world of philosophy, which also is called
forth by the ego, but now in the sense of the "transcendental ego."
These distinctions are based on certain, very specific views of the
connection existing between those worlds.

In the first place, we must ask how the lower and the higher
world are related. Isn't it obvious that the higher world is the
foundation of the lower world? Isn't God the foundation of
creation? The Christian philosophy of the Middle Ages had no
doubt about this matter. But at the beginning of the modern era
Descartes asked himself: How do I know that? I know it on the
basis of my faith, but I should not have recourse to my faith when I
really wish to function as a philosopher. As a philosopher I must
provisionally "suspend" all certainties that have not yet been se-
cured—and this includes my knowledge of God and the world—in
order to search for an indubitable starting point. Descartes found
this starting point in his *cogito*: "I think; therefore, I am." This
means that the higher world of the *cogito*, the world of "clear and
distinct ideas," as Descartes further specifies, becomes the basis
supporting all our knowledge, including that of the everyday
world.

Now, Husserl showed that this view is not right, at least not with
respect to the higher world of science. Physical science presupposes
experiments, and these demand a complex apparatus. But it is an
incontrovertible fact that the results of an experiment must be read
on the meters of the apparatus. Now, reading is something which I
do as an everyday human being. I would not even know what
science speaks about if I did not live in the everyday world of life.
This life-world, then, is a presupposition of science. Husserl, therefore, concluded that the oft-forgotten life-world is the foundation of
science.[8]

---

[8] Husserl, *Die Krisis der Europäischen Wissenschaften . . . , Husserliana*,
vol. VI, The Hague, 1954, par. 9h; cf. par. 33 and par. 34d.

Husserl's higher world, we said, is twofold. We have seen how the life-world and the higher world of science are related, but what is the relationship between the life-world and philosophy? Before we can answer this question, we must first describe the characteristics of the life-world.

I, this human being, one of the many people who live in the natural attitude, experience the world as "surrounding world" (*Umwelt*). This does not mean that I experience only a part of the world. In a certain sense I am conscious of the whole world. But the whole world can never be equally present to me in all its parts. I would have to stand outside the world for that, but as a matter of fact I stand in the midst of the world. It is this being in the midst of the world that is expressed by the term "surrounding world": the world is always around me, it has its center in me. Take, for example, the spatial structure of the world. When I perceive something, the object of my perception is always surrounded by a field of perception. This field, in its turn, is surrounded by a "circle" (*Umring*) of co-present things, things which I do not now perceive but of which I am aware anyhow. This circle itself is surrounded again by a vaguely conscious horizon of indeterminate reality. All this together is the world. Accordingly, the world, as my natural "surrounding world," is arranged in concentric circles around me as its center.

The life-world, then, is dependent on me. But it is characteristic of the life-world that it also shows a second feature which is diametrically opposed to the first. If I wish to describe the life-world in an adequate way, I must also say: I find the world "already there" and in this world I find many objects as pre-given. Whether I busy myself with them or not, the things are there, they are "present at hand" (*vorhanden*). In other words, they are prior to my turning to them, they are "ahead of me." But I find also myself within this world; I am an element of the world. Precisely as a link of the totality of the world, I am a man, I have a psyche, I am a natural ego.[9]

Thus the life-world is, on the one hand, dependent on me and, on the other, not dependent on me. Moreover, we must say that

[9] Cf. M. Theunissen, *Der Andere*, Berlin, 1965, Vol. I, Sect. I, Ch. I.

the natural ego gives preference to the independence of the world
from me, and so do the sciences. Science renounces all dependence
on the ego, it refuses admittance to all subjectivity, for it wishes to
be objective. Husserl, however, does not agree with this preference
of the natural attitude and views the objectivity of science as a
naive objectivity. His reason is that he does not wish to jeopardize a
truth brought to light by Descartes, viz., the truth that the ego, the
cogito is the source of the *meaning* of the world. The ego, says
Husserl, is characterized by intentionality and as such it gives the
world its *meaning*. This point becomes evident only when one
performs the operation which Husserl calls the "phenomenological
reduction." In this operation the dependence of the world on the
ego is made radical. The ego on which the meaning of the world is
radically dependent is called the "transcendental ego" because it no
longer contains any element of "experience." Science, then, finds its
foundation in the life-world, but the meaning of the life-world is
founded on the meaning-giving ego. Ultimately, therefore, the
(transcendental) ego is the origin of the meaning.

This thesis can be found in all phenomenologists, but in two
ways, viz., as a conviction and, at the same time, as a problem. The
fact that contemporary man has this conviction is not surprising, for
he has become conscious of his autonomy and therefore realizes
that he is the origin of his own world. Besides, he has become
sensitive to historicity: every man occupies a place of his own in
history and therefore every man sees the world in his own way.

At the same time, however, he is conscious of the fact that
unanswered questions are contained in this conviction. So far as
Christians are concerned, this consciousness usually arises from
their faith: if man is a creature, he has been placed in an order
which originates from God and not from man. But if there is a
problem here, the philosopher must solve it in a philosophical way.
For this reason it is important to note that the phenomenologists
themselves are conscious of the problematic aspect of their conviction. For instance, Merleau-Ponty points out that every reflection
must begin by returning to the life-world, as Husserl had rightly
demanded. But in that case the life-world cannot possibly have
totally originated in the transcendental ego; if the life-world was a

product of the ego, it would be wholly transparent to the ego, just as a product is known to its producer. But in that case it would not be necessary and even superfluous to return to the life-world. Moreover, as a matter of fact, the life-world is not transparent, but rather a darkness in which we can throw only a partial light. One who claims that the life-world is transparent lapses into the intellectualism of "contemplation." And, then, what possible sense could history still have? Human reflection is a reflection on something not reflected upon, which can never be totally encompassed by reflection.[10]

The problem involved in all this, we think, can be solved only within a hermeneutic philosophy. With phenomenology hermeneutic philosophy accepts that man is characterized by intentionality and that human intentionality assume the form of a "project." All achievements and acquisitions of the past are present in man because man is "thrown" into an environment in which these achievements play a role. This is why the hermeneutic situation needs to be more closely analyzed. The preferred model in which the hermeneutic situation can be disclosed is the attitude which a a reader assumes in reference to a text. It is in this hermeneutic perspective that the following chapters have been written.

---

[10] Merleau-Ponty, *Phenomenology of Perception*, New York, 1962, pp. 365, footnote (critique on Husserl), and X (reflection).

CHAPTER TWO

Devaluation Of The Immutable Truth

The mentality of the conservative thinker manifests itself in a typical way in the complaint that "instead of [adhering to] an absolute, fixed, unchangeable truth, some people practice a kind of relativism according to which truth is subject to the rhythm of evolution and of history."[1] The issue, then, is the opposition between fixed and immutable truth, on the one hand, and truth which evolves because it is involved in history, on the other. More specifically we will have to ask how this opposition should be understood. This question requires that we first describe how our evaluation of the fixed character of truth has changed; next, we will indicate some of the background of this change in appreciation.

1. The Fixed Standpoint

The topic of the fixed character of truth is typically Greek. To the best of my knowledge, it was first expressed by Plato in a philosophical context, which was mainly criteriological. But it was concerned with questions that touched the Greek concept of life and norms. At stake was Protagoras' thesis that man is the measure of all things. This thesis itself reflected the crisis affecting the Greek world-view during the transition from myth to logos. This

---

[1] Text of one of Cardinal Ottaviani's questions addressed to the bishops of The Netherlands, published in *Katholiek Archief*, October 7, 1966. For the answer of the bishops, see *Volkskrant*, December 29, 1967.

crisis was probably not caused by the sophists, but at least they gave expression to it and thereby accelerated the process of transition. They voiced doubt about the then current convictions. This doubt extended to the Greek world of gods but also to the accepted morality. The Greeks began to realize that every people has its own gods and its own customs. Didn't this mean, then, that man stands at the origin of his gods and of all his customs? Isn't man the measure of all things?

Socrates' action was fundamentally connected with this process of transition. According to Aristotle, Socrates discovered "the universal." The priest Euthyphro, a representative of the old, untouched magical-mythical faith, knows what piety is. Pious is, he says, what I am doing now, namely, accusing my own father of murder before the judge because he unwittingly let a slave starve to death. But Socrates is not satisfied with this answer. The issue is not whether this deed is pious or whether a whole series of deeds are pious. The question at stake is: what feature is to be found in all *pious* deeds and always remains *identical with itself?* what is the *piety* of all pious deeds?

Plato then put down this conviction in his *Cratylus* dialogue. The individual man is not the measure of all things. This is evident from the fact that we consider some people more expert than others. For what makes a man an expert is the fact that he is well versed in the matter under discussion. This means that this matter can be known, and the reason why it can be known is that it has a *permanent essence*. One can learn about this permanent essence; and some people have made more progress in this knowledge than others. We must conclude, then, that pious deeds can differ from one another, but they do not differ in piety; things change, but the essence of things does not change. "Things have a permanent essence of their own."[2]

In this way the danger of relativism was overcome for Socrates and Plato. The mythical certainties are gone, but this doesn't mean that everything has become unhinged. The logos, too, has its own anchor and therefore also its own certainties.

---

[2] *Cratylus*, 386a.

Permanence, fixity, then, is positively appreciated. This becomes evident when we examine the other terms and ideas with which the topic of permanence is connected in the Greek context. Permanence, in the sense of firmness, pertains to the earth in contrast to the fickleness of the water in the all-encompassing sea. Permanence belongs to a friendship which lasts and endures while the years go by. Permanence, in the sense of solidity, pertains to a testimony that is certain. Permanence stands particularly in contrast to the phantasy in which we let things run their course according to our wishes and fancies; permanence is connected with the hard truth of reality. Solidity and permanence go together, they constitute a value. For this reason permanence is a source of rest, just as phantasy is a source of unrest. Permanence is a guarantee against change. And because change implies impurity, permanence is pure, unmixed and genuine. The value of permanence, fixity, clearly manifests itself in the motion of the stars, in their fixed and regular orbits. These orbits can be mathematically calculated. And didn't science, which is man's highest power, originate from the most divine part of man? The immutable fixity and purity of the orbits run by the stars bear witness to their divinity.[3]

Precisely this thought, we think, should be seen against the background of a world not yet dominated by man, a world that is capricious, strange, threatening and hostile, a world which again and again overwhelms man because he does not yet have power over it. In such a world permanence is man's only support. On the basis of this positive appreciation, permanence, now localized in the essence of things, could begin to function as the pillar against which the waves of relativism are smashed.

Plato has also given philosophical expression to the topic of error. The Idea is related to the things of this world as the permanent is related to the errant. This expressed his conviction that mutability can only be understood as error. To err is that form of movement which no longer knows its starting point and is unable to find its ending point. For this reason Plato associates error with being-

---

[3] Cf. the author's book, *Ousia in de dialogen van Plato*, Leiden, 1961, pp. 39-40.

confused, dizziness, drunkenness. Within this context truth lacks all
motion because it has already arrived at its terminus and is fixed
and permanent, while error lacks all orientation to truth because
error is without any orientation. Moreover, precisely because it
lacks any idea of direction, error shows a multitude of movements,
it goes this way and that. For Plato multiplicity and error go
together. That's why unity pertains to truth, and plurality to error.
Any pluriformity of truth would be something unintelligible, a
contradiction in terms. Any pluriformity means uncertainty, and
the realm of uncertainty is the realm in which we argue with one
another.[4] In this way also pluriformity is a loss of unity; the latter
apparently is conceivable only as a closed front.

This conception—with its obvious background of man as a being
who, lacking a firm grip on nature, is at the mercy of its caprices—
was largely taken over by Christian thought and, in particular, by
Scholasticism. For Augustine immutability is the divine attribute
par excellence; hence the immutability of truth can function as a
proof for the existence of God. For Thomas Aquinas being is by its
very essence "like something fixed and established in nature,"
something beyond erroneous uncertainty, for it is figured out, established, certain and valid. It is of less importance here, however,
that the Greek conception continued to influence the Middle Ages
than that our appreciation of permanence and fixity has changed in
a negative sense.

2. *History May Not Be Immobilized*

In this matter Hegel is the antipode of Plato. The first philosopher
of history, Hegel is, so far as I know, also the first thinker who
defended the view that the fixed concepts should "be made fluid."
Fluidity begins to replace fixity. I take it for granted that this
development is connected with man's growing maturity and his
growing confidence in physical science, through which hitherto
unreliable nature could be increasingly brought under control.
What is striking, at any rate, is that the image of a stream, which
for the Greek Heraclitus was the image *par excellence* of mobility,

---

[4] *Op cit.,* pp. 94-96.

now receives a positive appreciation. Not only the valuation of permanence and fixity but also that of change are transformed into their opposites. This, too, is manifest in Hegel. Change is no longer simply understood as aberration; there is a direction in its movement, it is a movement toward a goal.

The Greeks, Hegel held, could not arrive at such a view because they stood at the beginning of Western history and the direction in which the movement went became evident only later in history. But then it appeared that everything real is rational and that the forms of the spirit which, as a matter of fact, did occur had to occur. Change is not an aberration but a development, a development toward self-consciousness and freedom. But this insight can only be reached if one's eyes are open to the continuous stream of events. The judging intellect cannot reach this insight; it breaks up the totality because only in this way can it get a grip on reality. This will to power, however, ends in utter chaos. We must give up this will to power. The primacy should not be assigned to the judging intellect and its truth of the judgment. "Truth lies in the totality." That's why the fixed concepts, in which reality is broken up, must be "made fluid." Truth and totality belong together, as do totality and development. Truth is an event.[5]

The philosophy of Henri Bergson is in dialogue with the idea of evolution of Charles Darwin and Herbert Spencer. These two sharpened his attention to development. But development is something which we most readily observe in ourselves. I am inclined to say that I change all the time because I continually pass over from one disposition to another; for example, first I was happy but now I am sad. But in that case I speak of my dispositions as if they constituted a block; while I *say* that I change, I see this change only as a transition from one disposition to another. This is an illusion, arising from the fact that my attention fluctuates.

On closer inspection I observe that my condition also is continually changing. Even when I look at one and the same object from one and the same standpoint, my seeing is at every moment a moment older than before. That's why change is continuous; time is

---

[5] Hegel, *Phänomenologie des Geistes*, ed. by Hermann Glockner, Stuttgart, 1951, pp. 11-66, 372-459.

the "stuff" out of which my being is made. I am a past which goes forward, thus consuming the future and becoming richer in the process. Every moment is something unforeseeable, a new creation, an original moment of a no less original history. The intellect, however, which forms concepts and judgments is not adapted to such a reality. The intellect forms words and concepts in juxtaposition, a series of immovable images which by their fast succession cause the illusion of movement, as is done by a movie. But the understanding intellect does not reach the reality of the movement; only intuition can do this.[6]

Phenomenology is primarily a revolt against immobility. Phenomenologists oppose fixed permanence because they think that man cannot have a history, cannot be creative if he is locked up in a universe whose structures are prefixed. What is permanent is now understood as anything that no longer is fluid but has been made fast and therefore is fixed. And fixation is viewed as a violation of the dignity pertaining to creative man.

The fact that fixed permanence has lost its attraction is also connected with the Freudian insight that man cannot be reduced to his consciousness. Within the exclusive domain of consciousness fixed stability could be positively appreciated, but this is no longer possible when one knows about the margin surrounding consciousness, the margin out of which consciousness receives its nourishment. From this standpoint fixation is a defect. The newspaper which published the Report mentioned at the beginning of this chapter referred to Ottaviani's fixism. Human life is a drama that may not be brought to a standstill. Life is a drama, action, history. It ceases to be authentically human life when it stagnates and stops moving, when one thinks that the final stage has already been reached. There is no final stage within human life. Life is a meaningful wandering, which knows and does not know of a final stage because it is a knowing consciousness and, at the same time, a not-knowing margin, a searching and groping knowing which needs trial and error. Fixed immobility is a pretense or rather an illusion,

---

[6] Bergson, *L'évolution créatrice*, éd. du Centenaire, Paris, 1959, pp. 495-500, 623-635.

an intellectual precipitate of an existential estrangement, an alienation from the reality of being-human. Man must remain mobile;
any kind of immobility is a defect.

That is why permanence in the sense of immutability, immobility and fixation—is viewed as rigidity and petrifaction. And once it
is understood in this way, permanence gives rise to a whole string
of negative appreciations. What is rigid or petrified is unadapted.
What is at stake here is not primarily a matter of social adaptation.
Adaptation cannot be an absolute ideal because it would exclude
that I could ever exercise influence on society's development. Rigidity is primarily unadapted to my own life history because it
prevents me from being open to the unexpected "moment" in the
events that happen to me. Whatever has become rigid and petrified is by the very fact no longer a part of my life. To the extent
that I have become petrified, I myself have dropped out of my own
life. Rigidity belongs to the realm of death—don't we speak of *rigor
mortis?*—and contradicts initiative, which literally means the making of a new beginning.

My life ought not to run a course outside my own initiative. Any
life should retain the freedom in truth to bring itself about. In
every life the own truth about its own life must come about. That's
why this truth, which is the first sense of truth, is an event. That's
also why this truth has as many forms as there are human beings,
and why a uniform truth is just as objectionable as a standardized
humanity. No relativism is implied in this assertion, as we will see.
For no one determines for himself who he *authentically* is. Life is a
laborious groping precisely because I wish to become who I am,
without knowing as yet who I authentically am, save by way of an
anticipating surmise. One who in this way gives up the easy
anchorage of immobility and surrenders to what happens to him, in
an attitude which a believer would call Christian, puts his trust in
the meaningfulness of life's history.

Finally, isn't it true that contemporary man, in spite of everything, also continues positively to appreciate fixed permanence in a
certain sense? We value a regular job or a profession with a regular
salary; we value a regular pension, preferably one whose purchas-
ing power is securely fixed. We struggle for social security as a

right for everyone because we think that socio-economic insecurity must be taken away if a man is to have an opportunity to develop himself genuinely as a man. But it should be noted that the fixed character involved in these things is not a good pursued as an end but only as a means.

3. The Changed View of Man

Does all this mean that there are no longer any permanent truths for one who is willing to bring about his own history and his own part of the world's history? As was pointed out above, faithfulness to history does not at all imply the fatal consequence of relativism. In the course of the following chapters this point will be considered more extensively. By way of conclusion for this chapter we merely wish to add the following remarks.

Fixed permanence—the immutable essence and immutable truth —functioned as the ideal that arose during the transition from myth to logos. Truth is still the ideal today, but now no longer as immutable truth. The fact that the immutable truth has been driven from its supreme position is connected with the fact that the logos, i.e. the judging intellect, no longer functions as the supreme ideal. There is room for this logos in the new picture of man, but it no longer holds the primacy.

The picture of man has changed, as we saw in Chapter One. *Theoria* or contemplation was the philosophy which had withdrawn from everyday life and occupied itself exclusively with the higher world of the Idea and of essence. Immutable truth was the supreme ideal of that contemplation; and this did not cause any difficulties because, by withdrawing from the lower world, contemplation had also lost change and development.

What is the picture of man presented by a philosophy that wishes to be contemplation? Man is a soul, an intellect, and therefore Socrates says that he is concerned with the soul and the truth. It must be admitted, of course, that Aristotle no longer called man a soul; moreover, Thomas Aquinas offered an impressive defense of the unity of body and soul. But, in spite of this, neither Aristotle nor Aquinas managed to draw the consequences from the unity of body and soul for the unity of man's knowledge. Besides, since

Marx knowledge or contemplation is no longer the supreme ideal. On the other hand, *praxis* cannot take the place of *theoria* or contemplation because *praxis* itself presupposes insights.

That is why the phenomenologist says that both *theoria* and *praxis* are splits from a prior unity which is the origin of knowing and striving, valuing and acting. This unity lies in human intentionality (Husserl) or, in Heidegger's words, that unity is man as project. Man accomplishes his history by breaking open the "thrownness" which he is in a project that is both a self-project and a project of the world. The expression that man is a project means that he is not fixed, he forces open what has already been fixed, established. In this opening of the established, man brings about his history. But because the self-project is at the same time a project of the world, it also breaks open the world and makes the world come about. The philosophy of contemplation disregards the fundamental fact that man is *not primarily* a contemplator of the world nor primarily a contemplator of essences, but the being who humanizes himself and the world.

Thus man, as project, is that movement in which the facticity of his own ego and of the world is transcended and reaches forward toward a new possibility, one which presently will become the new shape of the ego and of the world and then, in its turn, will again be transcended. Man is primarily a "transcending movement" (Merleau-Ponty). Secondarily, however, man continues to find it necessary to form universal concepts and make universal statements. These statements derive their meaning from the transcending movement which man is; they must remain within the context of this movement as clarifying expressions of the things already attained within this movement but not yet put into words. If statements cut themselves off from the movement, they become petrified. History is both development and renewal; outside history there is only petrifaction. "We have no other choice than that between renewal and petrifaction."[7]

How the relationship between the human project and human statements must be determined is a matter that will be clarified later. Similarly, the question of how the project attains truth is still to be discussed, in particular in Chapter Five. For the present we

---

[7] Lenten pastoral of the Dutch Bishops, 1968.

may conclude that man has two possibilities at his disposal. As a transcending movement, man is progressive, just as for Marx the proletarian, who holds the future in his hands, is progressive. To the extent that man isolates his universal concepts and judgments from the transcending movement which he himself is, sets them apart and fixes them, he is conservative. This statement is meant to be philosophical. Only when this philosophical statement is made can the psychological question be raised why certain people feel and think in a distinctly conservative way while others do it in a clearly progressive fashion. This psychological question will not be examined in this book, for we are concerned with a philosophical investigation.

CHAPTER THREE

Totalitarian Or Individual Arbitrariness?

In Chapter One we argued that since Marx it is no longer possible to dismiss the so-called lower world and withdraw to the world of Ideas or essences. For it is in the lower world that human individuals live and it is there that history runs its course. Contemporary thought is characterized by an increased sensitivity to historicity and individuality. In the preceding chapter we have presented a few points expressing our view of historicity and the consequences historicity has for man's concept of truth. We must now indicate the development toward greater attention to individuality. While the Greeks preferred the species to the individual, contemporary man assigns priority to the individual over the species. What is the line along which this idea has developed?

The problem of individual and species constitutes the main topic of a previous publication by the author,[1] but what follows here is not a summary of that work. The metaphysical aspects of species and individual are largely omitted here. Let us begin with Diotima, the woman who in Plato's *Symposium* revealed to Socrates what love is.

1. Immortality Through Reproduction

All people desire the good in order to be happy through its possession. But it is not enough to say that all people desire to

---

[1] *Op zoek naar identiteit*, Utrecht, 1958.

possess the good; they wish to have it *forever*. How is that possible since man is mortal and the brief duration of his life conflicts with this "forever"? Let us abstract from love in the broader sense and pay attention to sexual love and procreation. As soon as we have reached a certain age, our nature tends to procreate. The grandeur of this event demands beauty, for deformity is ill suited to it. This event is grand because it is divine. And what is the divine aspect of this event? "To the mortal creature, generation is a sort of eternity and immortality." Man wishes to possess the good *forever* although he is mortal. This is possible because he is immortal through procreation.

That's why even animals will starve to feed their offspring and are ready to die in defense of their young. For the mortal nature in them seeks "as far as possible to be everlasting and immortal." But it can attain this only through procreation, for then a new existence takes the place of the old. This succession of the new on the old can be observed even in one and the same individual: the child becomes adult, and the adult becomes old. In this process man changes in every respect—hair, flesh, blood as well as habits, desires and even thoughts are changing. Yet we say that he remains the same. In this way the mortal partakes of immortality. Only God stays the same by remaining forever unchanged. The mortal is preserved because that which disappears and becomes old leaves behind a new being of the same kind as the old. Through this mechanism the mortal partakes of the immortal.[2]

This passage contains no less than three decisions; they are concerned with the meaning of sexual intercourse, death, and individuality. Sexual intercourse is connected with procreation; the death of the individual is minimized by referring to the offspring in which one continues to live; and the individual is subordinated to his nature. These decisions are interconnected. The primary position of nature is fundamental; our nature tends to procreate, our mortal nature wishes to be immortal. The starting point of the passage was broader; it was still concerned with concrete human beings, all of whom desire the good. But this starting point got lost in the discourse. That's why procreation is considered a kind of

---

[2] *Symposium*, 206c-208b.

"mechanism"; no matter what intentions concrete human beings may attach to their sexual intercourse, nature reaches its goal independently of them and even against them.

It stands to reason that the high mortality of those days played a role in this approach. At a time when the population increase is small or non-existent, one can envision the possibility that the human race will die out. But this possibility is not a satisfactory explanation. For the issue is not only the continuation of the human race but also the individual man who in his progeny attains immortality. And what is involved here is the relationship of the individual to the human race. Now, as we saw, the individuality of each man is reduced to something trivial here. Just as the individual changes during his life, so also do individuals change from one to another. Man remains the same throughout the changes occurring in his life; likewise, man remains the same in the changes from one individual to another. But the man who remains the same in the changes affecting his life is *this* man, this individual. The man, on the other hand, who remains the same when the individuals change is an entirely different man. What should we call him? Taking up Plato's idea, Aristotle offers us an answer.

Reproduction, Aristotle points out, is the most natural act of a living being. It produces a being similar to itself, a plant producing a plant, an animal an animal, "in order that, as far as its nature allows, it may partake in the eternal and the divine." But no perishable being can partake in the eternal by uninterrupted continuance; therefore, it tries to attain that end in the only possible way: "it remains not indeed as the self-same individual but continues its existence in something like itself—not numerically but specifically one."[3]

The man who remains the same in the succession of individuals is not numerically the same but specifically one; it is "the" man. We know him, for we speak of him in definitions and statements such as "man is a rational animal." Individual man is subordinate to and less important than the species "man." For the sake of eternity and immortality man does everything his nature renders possible. But Aristotle himself points out that the expression "for the sake of" is

---

[3] *De anima*, bk. II, ch. 4; 415a 26-415b 7.

ambiguous; it means for the sake of eternity and immortality, but it also means "for the sake of nature," that is, for the benefit of nature.[4] If the individual lives for the benefit of nature, then we can understand that his death is unimportant and that sexual intercourse is a function in the service of procreation.

Why is there so little appreciation here for the concrete individual? Reaction to sophistry again is an important factor. The sophists put great emphasis on the individual, as should be evident from Protagoras' thesis that "man is the measure of all things," for, says Socrates, that thesis implies that "things are to you such as they appear to you, and to me such as they appear to me" (*Theaetetus*, 152a). This view, Socrates held, would put universally valid values in jeopardy. That is why individuality became a symbol of willfulness and arbitrariness.

Plato also did not write a philosophy of the individual ego. The citizens of his *Republic* must constitute a single body. Unity must be their supreme good, dividedness the supreme evil. As soon as an individual citizen calls something "mine," that unity would be broken; only that which is common to all may be "mine."[5] Man shouldn't let himself be guided by his personal desires, but should become like the fixed and immutable essence of things, for this essence is the same for everyone. Only in this way can arbitrariness be avoided. One who strives for the genuine values must disregard his individuality. There is no room in this perspective for the view that the differences between individual men could be important or that immortality pertains to the individual human being. While Plato recognizes the immortality of the human soul, this immortality does not imply "an immortalization of the individual in the soul."[6]

We saw that Aristotle calls the man who remains in the succession of the individuals "specifically the same." The "species" man is man insofar as man has the "essence" of man—the Greek term *eidos* means both species and essence. All human beings and only they possess the human essence; it is this that determines the

---

[4] *Ibid.*, 415b 2-3.
[5] *Republic*, 462a-466; cf. *Symposium*, 205e.
[6] J. Stenzel, *Metaphysik des Altertums*, München, 1931, p. 114.

human species. Now, Aristotle shares Plato's view of individuality. The essence common to all men is what is good in man, it is his positive aspect. This becomes clear when I express the fixed essence of man in a judgment. For in the definition thus obtained the verbal copula "is" implies absolute identity. This should be evident from the fact that this judgment can be read from left to right as well as from right to left: "man is a rational animal" or "the rational animal is a man." Now, absolute identity is divine, pure and unmixed.

The differences between human beings arise from so-called individuating matter. But matter is the negative element in man. This shows itself in the fact that matter can give rise to an unlimited plurality of differences, cannot be understood by man and causes man to be subject to corruption. Because of matter, the individual man is not at one with his essence, he can act in a way that disagrees with his essence and pursue his own private interest. Individuality is a defect with respect to the fullness and the goodness of the species. That is why for Aristotle also it is unthinkable that the individual man—or even the individual soul—would be immortal, except for the spirit, which could exist outside the individual just as it has entered man "from without."[7]

Accordingly, Aristotle's theory of matter and form implies that the primacy belongs to the species and not to the individual, because the primacy belongs to the fixed and immutable truth and not to the individual standpoint. If the individual differences are not important, the terrifying conclusion follows of necessity that individuals are interchangeable and can replace one another. In this line of thinking an individual is nothing but a *random* and therefore *replaceable sample* of the *species*.

The Christian philosophers of the Middle Ages had not yet learned to see the dimension of historicity; they therefore held fast to the primacy of fixed and immutable truth. Thus they had also to hold fast to the primacy of the species. But this also produced a tension within the sphere of their faith. For God's concern goes out to the individual, whom He knows from within and in his very depth:

---

[7] *De generatione animalium*, 736b 27.

O Lord, you have probed me and you know me;
you know when I sit and when I stand;
you understood my thoughts from afar. . . .
Behind me and before, you hem me in
and rest your hand upon me.
Such knowledge is too wonderful for me;
too lofty for me to attain. (Ps. 138, 1-2, 6)

And where God is known as the Father, so that the believers in
Him are His children, the relationship between God and man is a
personal relationship as between individual persons. In this perspective the individual can no longer be replaceable, for love is
directed to him precisely as this individual man. Nevertheless, the
Christian thinkers of the Middle Ages were on guard not to open
the door to individual willfulness and arbitrariness. That's why they
held fast to the Greek framework ascribing the primacy to the
species. The tension that arose in this way between their thinking
and their faith was de-emphasized as much as possible. An un-
sound proposal was, as it were, on the agenda, but one that could
not be rejected; so they limited themselves to amending it as much
as possible.

Thomas Aquinas, for example, never showed any hesitation in his
conviction that God has a perfect knowledge of the individual. This
was a victory over Plato and Aristotle. At the same time, he
recognized that the individual soul is immortal, in support of which
he often used an improved version of Diotima's argument: because
the intellect is directed to "to be," without the limitation of the here
and now, it naturally desires "to be forever" and this natural desire
cannot be in vain.[8] But Aquinas continued to affirm that the
goodness of the species transcends that of the individual, that the
individuals exist for the sake of the species, and that God's intentions are principally concerned with the species. The species, he
said, is "more virtuous" than the individual.[9] This statement indicates that for him also the individual is marked by a lack of virtue,
by willfulness and arbitrariness. In a word, Aquinas did not solve

[8] *Summa theologica*, p. I, q. 75, a.6c.
[9] *In "De coelo et mundo,"* bk. I, lect. 19 (no. 197 in Marietti ed.), *Contra genter,* bk. III, ch. 59.

the problem of individuality, but he made a contribution to its solution when he said that *being* and *being-individual* mean the same.[10]

2. In Death the Species Obtains a Victory

In the preceding chapter we said that Hegel was the first philosopher bearing witness to a modern feeling for historicity. The name of Marx could have been added to that of Hegel. But if we ask if these two thinkers have been of importance for the positive appreciation of individuality, the answer must be that, appearances to the contrary, this was in fact hardly the case.

To begin with Hegel, his emphasis on the value of a few historical figures is well known. For example, Socrates, Descartes and Napoleon; particularly Antigone is for him the most sublime figure who ever appeared on earth. It is also true that for Hegel abstract universality is no ideal; only through particularization and individuality does abstract universality develop into the concretely universal. Plato, we said above, opted for the primacy of the species, but Hegel reproaches Plato for disregarding the individual and wrongly denying man property and a family of his own.[11] Hegel praises Christianity because it recognized the infinite value of the individual.

All this means that Hegel does indeed ascribe a certain value to the individual; the "world-historical individual" has been a factor for him in the development of the Spirit toward self-consciousness and freedom. For the Spirit increasingly comes to itself by finding itself in everything which at first opposes itself as a foreign power to consciousness. This development of the Spirit—or at least *to* the Spirit—is the central topic of Hegel's thought. But precisely in this, Hegel's ultimate concern is not with the individual in the sense of this unrepeatable human being, circumscribed by his own limits.

For this philosophy of the Spirit is characterized by a twofold protest. In the first place, it is a protest against Kant's philosophy of finiteness and against any form of thought that wishes to lock man

---

[10] Cf. the author's work *Op zoek naar identiteit*, pp. 130-140.
[11] Hegel, *Grundlinien der Philosophie des Rechts*, ed. Hoffmeister, par. 185 and 206.

up again in his finiteness. God must again become the beginning of philosophy, says Hegel,[12] but for him God is not an infinite being alongside and above the finite beings. The statement that God must be the beginning of philosophy means that the true philosophy—Hegel's own—must overcome the opposition between the finite and the infinite (between *Diesseits* and *Jenseits*). Finite man must become infinite, and the infinite Spirit must become finite. One process with two aspects is involved here, and this process runs its course in history.

The individual man, however, is an incomplete spirit. Insofar as he is *spirit* and, therefore, oriented to the universal, he transcends all limitations, even the ultimate limit of death itself, for the spiritual is not perishable. But this doesn't mean an individual continuation of existence. For precisely as an individual, man is an *incomplete* spirit, and the incomplete has no right to an independent existence. Only that which is complete exists by its own power; the incomplete *is* only a "moment" of what exists of necessity, a moment of a certain duration, mortal and perishable. The death of the individual man is an absolute necessity.

Thus it is the task of man to do justice to the incomplete spirit which he is. That's why he may not use his individuality as a barrier between his incomplete spirituality and the complete spirituality to which he must contribute his share. This leads to Hegel's second protest, viz., against Romanticism and, in it, against the individual who would appeal to his uniqueness. True, Christianity is right when it ascribes an infinite value to the individual, for the Spirit needs the incomplete spirits for its development. But this does not mean that individuality could constitute a source of knowledge, as is wrongly asserted by the Romanticists.

Hegel continually fulminates against the Romantic passion for originality. "Evil" is for him identical with "the arbitrariness which prefers one's own particularity to the universal."[13] An opinion, then is more original according as it is more evil. In this respect Romanticism does not differ from Greek sophistry. Hegel speaks of the superficial principles of sophistry which we know about from

---

[12] *Wie der gemeine Menschenverstand die Philosophie nehme,* in Hegel Studien-Ausgabe (Fischer Bücherei), vol. 1, p. 86.
[13] *Grundlinien der Philosophie des Rechts,* par. 139 and 317.

Plato's works, principles "which base right" and truth "on subjective intentions and opinions, on subjective sentiment and private conviction."[14] Hegel despises and hates those principles because they go counter to man's nature; man, he holds, is precisely as a thinking being, from the very start an (abstract) universality and must use his individuality to make his universality concrete.

All this shows that ultimately Hegel's position does not differ from that of Plato; he, too, knows only a choice between individual willfulness or arbitrariness and, on the other hand, a universality that is ultimately *the same for all men*. Hegel, too, doesn't yet see the possibility of an individual approach to truth that is really individual and, at the same time, does not cease to be truth.

This makes it necessary for us to return to the matter discussed in the preceding chapter. As we saw there, Hegel recognized the dimension of historicity. He accepts therefore that truth is in development and he rejects the fixed and immutable truth. This means that a truth-conflict can arise between a person who has already reached a higher level and others who still remain on a lower level. This situation is interesting in connection with the discussion between conservatives and progressives. Hegel refers specifically to Socrates. This thinker had reached a higher level of consciousness than his contemporaries. That's why he was right in his resistance to the traditional gods of the city of Athens. His resistance was ethically justified; Socrates had no right to act otherwise than he did. But the judges who condemned him were also right from their level; they were justified in condemning him. Such a situation is for Hegel eminently tragic.

In Hegel's opinion, however, no matter how easily a truth-conflict can arise between people living on different levels, such a conflict is impossible with respect to individuals living on the same level of development. For, as far as Hegel is concerned, it is excluded that the unrepeatable individual can be an authentic source of insight. That, nevertheless, he is such a source will be discussed in the following chapters; here we merely wish to indicate the background of Hegel's position. This background evidently is the idea that all oppositions, in particular that between the finite and the

---

14 *Ibid.*, Einleitung, p. 11.

infinite and between individuality and universality, must be transcended.[15]

At the same time, our objection to that opposition should be obvious. The boundaries between the individuals should not be wiped out for the sake of universality or for the sake of the species. The nefarious consequences of Hegel's faulty position are disclosed by the history of Europe, its inquisitions, its Stalinism and two world wars. This is a point repeatedly emphasized by Emmanuel Levinas. Besides, insofar as man is concerned, death is no victory of the species over the individual. Putting myself provisionally on a religious basis, I consider the individual invincible, for it is for the sake of him, and not of the species, that Christ has overcome death.

Did Marx manage to arrive at a clearer standpoint than Hegel with respect to individuality? As is well-known, Marx always criticized Hegel for his mystifications. While considering himself an interpreter of Hegel, Marx wished to bring Hegel to the truth by bringing him back to concrete reality. That's why he did not share Hegel's preference for the universal. Hegel spoke of the human species, and Marx is willing to to take this term over from him but only after stripping it of all its mystifications. Writing to Feuerbach he said: "If the concept of man-as-species is brought down from the 'heaven' of abstraction to the real earth, what else it is but the concept of society?"[16] The statement that man is part of the species, then, means that no totally isolated human individual is possible. Man always lives in a "society," and for Marx this term refers not merely to civil society but expresses primarily that "society" is human and that man is "social." Human beings are each other's partners.

Marx's central idea, however, is that this partnership has hitherto been realized only in an alienated way. All should take care of what is of interest to all; instead, people are divided into two classes, and the ruling class imposes on the other class the destiny of of being its servant. "The history of all hitherto existing society,"

---

[15] See footnote 12 and Hegel's *Logik*, Lasson ed., pp. 103-147.

[16] "Brief an Feuerbach," 11 Augustus, 1844, Karl Marx, *Texte zu Methode und Praxis*, vol. 2, RoRoRo ed., 1966, p. 185. See also *Thesen ad Feuerbach*, no. 6 (in *Selected Works*, vol. 2, p. 404).

says Marx at the beginning of his *Manifesto*, "is the history of class struggles." Because of this division into classes, it is impossible for either the proletarian or the capitalist to be fully human; they are divided from one another and, therefore, neither one nor the other can realize his social essence.

To the extent that he is estranged, then, every individual stands in an antagonistic attitude with respect to the human species. That is why every individual, the capitalist included, is poor because he is separated from the greatest wealth, viz., his fellowman. This kind of poverty is called egoism. An erroneous idea of freedom underlies egoism, namely, the idea that man, "as an isolated monad withdrawn into himself," is free because he has separated himself from his fellowman, whom he wrongly views as a limitation of his freedom. Egoism simply fails to appreciate that man can realize his freedom only through his fellowman. Man withdraws from his fellowman to himself and therefore to "his private interest and his private willfulness" and, consequently, also to "his private property."[17] Egoism ultimately is the egoism of private interests which has made man unfaithful to his own social nature, so that he is divided against himself.

What else follows from this than Hegel's conclusion that man must do justice to the universal—that is, social—being which he is? If Marx rises above Hegel in this matter, it is because he discovered the laws according to which one day the situation of man's estrangement will come to an end. This will come about, Marx holds, through the power of the proletariat. The bourgeoisie of necessity produces its own gravediggers; that's why its death and the victory of the proletariat are both inevitable. Yet, Marx holds, the proletarian consciousness is an integral part of this necessity; to this extent he retains the Hegelian demand that man must trancend his private interests, but he must do it by the power of the proletarian universality.

Finally, in the description of the definitive communist society we see in the most convincing way the return of Hegel's conviction that every opposition between individuality and universality must be transcended. The third of Marx's PARISIAN MANUSCRIPTS can serve

---

17 Cf. "On the Jewish Question," *Writings of the Young Marx on Philosophy and Society*, pp. 235f.

as an example. It is concerned with true communism and points out that the transcending of the alienation follows the same road as the alienation itself. Man's estrangement arose from the egoism of private interests and private property. Therefore, every division— every "separation" or "split," to use Marx's favored terms—will be transcended when private interests and private property are transcended. Man will then appropriate his total essence. He will return to himself as the social, the human man. Every struggle with fellowman, every conflict between individual and species will be overcome. What we will have to be particularly on guard against, says Marx, is to reestablish society as an abstraction *vis-à-vis* the individual. Individual life and species life are *not different*. In the sense of this unity communism is the solution of the riddle of history.[18]

Both Marx and Hegel are convinced that all opposition, duality or non-identity within man and between men must be overcome. The opposition implied in distinct individuality is intolerable. It is not surprising, therefore, that totalitarian tendencies exist in both thinkers and that these have led to ideas of the State or society in which no opposition can be tolerated. Besides, how is it possible to govern a State or society in which all people are equal? This is possible only because in this era, before the definitive communist era, some people have made greater progress in their proletarian consciousness than others; the latter, then, still live on a lower level. This brings to mind the case of Socrates, who rightly held fast to his conviction and who rightly also was condemned by the Athenian authorities. But in communist countries it happens rather frequently that those who are supposed to have reached a higher level of consciousness are precisely the people who are in power.

Marx says that the individual and the species constitute a unity. But the individual dies while the human species continues to exist. How does Marx solve this problem? "Death," he says, "seems to be a hard victory of the species over the particular individual and to contradict their unity. But the particular individual is only a partic-

---

[18] "Private Property and Communism," *Economic and Philosophical Manuscripts of 1844*, Moscow, 1961, p. 105.

ular species-being and, as such, is mortal."[19] In other words, there is only a pseudo-problem here. Marx continues to hold fast to the unity of the individual and the species, a unity that is not eliminated by death. For it is *this* man who dies and *this* man is *not* the individual, but *only* a particular species-being. In other words, when Marx speaks of the individual, he does not refer to *this* man. But for us *this* man is the only individual man. Marx appreciates *this* man negatively ("only"); *this* man receives from him the same negative appreciation as he got from Aristotle. For Marx the individual is a sample of the human species; all together and each one separately are such samples; any one can do and all are interchangeable. This is also Aristotle's idea of individuality, an idea that remained active in the Middle Ages and active also in Hegel and Marx.

3. Orientated to Death, Man Becomes an Individual

Although Schleiermacher, Nietzsche and Kierkegaard had even earlier shown increased sensitivity to the irreplaceable ownness of the individual, it was only through Husserl's phenomenology that individuality fully received its true dimension. As we saw in Chapter One, Husserl argued against Descartes that science has its foundation in the life-world, but he retained what was true in Descartes by positing that the meaning of the life-world is founded on the meaning-giving ego. This ego Husserl calls the "transcendental ego." Now, if we wish to describe the transcendental ego, we must say that it is *"always mine"* (*jemeinig*) and *absolute*. These two characteristics contain a new appreciation of individuality. This is a point on which we must now reflect.

The life-world reveals a contradictory feature. On the one hand, it is always around me (*Umwelt*), I am its center; on the other, the life-world precedes me and I find myself in that world. In a similar way the other people also shows a contradictory feature. In the life-world that precedes me I find myself as a man among billions of people and my position as such is equal to that of all the

---

[19] *Ibid.*

other human beings. But this is no longer the case in the life-world as my "surrounding world" (*Umwelt*), for in this world I am the center. This means that the others are not in the center but in my surrounding world, and I am also their center.

Now, Husserl's transcendental philosophy radicalizes the ego-dependence of the world in the hope of remaining more faithful to the truth of Descartes than was Descartes himself. For man is characterized by intentionality and, consequently, he is the foundation of meaning. But the meaning arising from me lies around me. If I wish to understand this truth radically, I return to myself, but now to myself as transcendental ego. The transcendental ego, then, is my ego; for anyone who philosophizes it is his ego; it is "always mine" (*jemeinig*). But as the radicalization of the central ego, the transcendental ego doesn't know any equals. It itself is a subjectivity and it does not know any other subjects, for the others are still in its "surrounding world," so that they do not yet differ from objects; their subjectivity, therefore, is not yet known to the transcendental ego. Accordingly, the transcendental ego is the absolute subject, an "I" not opposed to a "you" and a "he"; as such it is *absolute*.

Accordingly, for each one his transcendental ego is absolute, a source of meaning welling up from the individual ego. Abandoning Husserl's terminology, we may translate this idea by saying that the ego, precisely as project, is a source of truth which cannot be brought to light by any other ego. This means that a truth-conflict is now possible, not merely between people on different levels of development, as was held by Marx and Hegel, but also between people within respect to whom a difference in level plays no role. We would even prefer to say that all people necessarily occupy a different standpoint, but that, too, would be a correction of Hegel.

At the end of Chapter One we noted that phenomenology gives rise to a problem to which some phenomenologists themselves appear to be sensitive, viz., the question whether the giving of meaning is or is not absolutely autonomous. This problem arises especially in the relationship of the ego to its fellowman. If the ego is a meaning-giving being, then, so it seems, the ego can encounter other people only as objects of its project, as what is projected by its project. But doesn't this mean that the ego then disregards the other as he is in himself? In that case the ego never reaches the other and can never found a genuine community with the other. This problem will be considered in Chapters Six and Eight; right now it is enough to realize the existence of this problem: the new approach, for which we have called upon phenomenology as a witness, an approach which, in principle, is a gain over any form of thought that makes the individual subordinate to the species and the universal essence, at first makes the other ego a problem. This problem manifests itself even in Heidegger although he seems to contradict our claim.

Husserl's transcendental ego, we saw, does not know equals. But Heidegger points out that in a "description" of the "surrounding world" we also encounter the others. The boat anchored near the shore refers me to a friend who likes to use it, or if it is a strange boat it refers to other people. We don't first see a boat and then add people to it in our thoughts. I only encounter the boat in terms of the world in which it is the other's boat, and that world is always also mine. In a word, the world is always the world which I share with others.

The question must be asked as to who these others are with whom I share the world. Heidegger's answer is that these others are not all other people in contrast to myself. On the contrary, they are those people from whom one doesn't usually distinguish oneself because one is one of them. But who is the one who usually doesn't distinguish himself from the others? That is someone who is not as the being which he himself is, one who is not himself because the others have robbed him of his being. In this situation everyone is the other and no one is himself. It is the situation of inauthenticity. The question, then, Who is it that doesn't distinguish himself from the others? must be answered by saying that it is the "neuter," the impersonal "one." And this "one" is "No one."[20]

The man, then, who shares the world with others as a matter of course is for Heidegger the inauthentic man, the one who has not yet come to himself. It makes sense to compare this man to Husserl's natural ego. Husserl's transcendental ego, however, is the ego

---

[20] Heidegger, *Sein und Zeit*, pp. 117-130.

that has come back to itself from the world in which it was lost. This transcendental ego must not be compared to the inauthentic man but to the authentic man. But what happens, according to Heidegger, to man's being-together-with-the-others (*Miteinandersein*) when man comes to his authenticity?

Because the inauthentic man is wholly submerged in the impersonal "one," he can come to authenticity only by liberating himself from the others' domination. This happens in an "individualization" (*Vereinzelung*), the one in which man "runs ahead" and anticipates his death. The inauthentic man avoids death; that's why he doesn't become himself. But I individualize myself as *this* man whom I authentically am when I realize that death is for me my ownmost possibility. No one can take my place in death. At the same time, I become disclosed to myself as the one who cannot be interchanged with anyone else.

With respect to death man is entirely thrown back upon his ownmost potentiality. All relationships with his fellowmen are cut off in this situation. But in this "individuation" I disclose myself in my authenticity. And this means that the authentic man, likewise, has broken off his relationships with other people. "All being-with-others fails us when our ownmost potentiality-for-being is the issue."[21]

Nevertheless, Heidegger explicitly says that only in my being my ownmost self can being-with-one-another become authentic. But how can a being-with-others be ascribed to the non-relational ego, especially if we realize that this ego is no less solitary than Husserl's transcendental ego? Heidegger merely answers that the man who has understood his ownmost potentiality understands at the same time that the other's possibilities are not his precisely because they are the ownmost possibilities of the other. There is no longer any risk that he will impose his possibilities on the other.[22]

The bond of the ego with the other, then, is no problem with respect to the inauthentic man, but it remains a problem, also in Heidegger, for the man who has disclosed his authenticity to himself. This problem will be discussed in Chapter Six in connection with estrangement; here we merely wished to note the existence of

---

[21] *Sein und Zeit*, p. 263.
[22] *Op. cit.*, p. 264.

this problem, which is relevant to the topic of this chapter. Our discussion of the relationship between species and individual shows that the primacy is ascribed either to the species or to the individual; and either position gives rise to a host of problems.

If the primacy is assigned to the universal essence and the species, one is in a position where he can call a halt to individual willfulness and arbitrariness. An appeal can be made to general rules and laws which restrain individual arbitrariness. But in this perspective it is no longer possible to see that individuality can be an authentic source of insight, for the unrepeatable individual and his history have been set aside. The individual can now occur only as a random and interchangeable sample of the species. In this way the door is opened for an arbitrariness that is not individual but totalitarian. Besides, one who rigidly adheres to the consequences of this perspective can, strictly speaking, no longer defend a personal immortality. In other words, this standpoint not merely makes the unrepeatable individual a problem; it compromises him beyond recall.

The alternative is to attribute the primacy to the individual as this unrepeatable and non-interchangeable man. There is then a possibility to value the history of the individual as the coming to pass of something in which a truth is disclosed that cannot be brought to light by anyone else. Totalitarian arbitrariness is excluded. Besides, the possibility of personal immortality reveals itself only here.[23] But this perspective also has serious difficulties. Personal willfulness and arbitrariness are not yet excluded. The value of universal statements and norms is relativized; even more strongly expressed, the question remains unanswered whether man's giving of meaning is subject to norms or wholly autonomous. Finally, the bond of the individual with the others becomes a problem, so that the threatening possibility of anarchy appears on the horizon. Whether or not these difficulties can be overcome is a question to be examined in the following chapters.

---

[23] I would start from the unique position of man as the only being whose ownness lies still ahead of him, the only being which has a *telos*, an end. This unique position can, I think, intelligibly be explained by saying that man is unique because everything else is mortal and he alone is immortal. Concerning the question of immortality, see Chapter Nine.

We are now in a position where a closer description of the progressive and the conservative man can be given than was possible at the end of the preceding chapter. We said that man is progressive as a transcending movement. Now we understand that one who does justice to the transcending movement which he is values individual history as the coming to pass of something in which a truth is disclosed that could not be disclosed in any other individual. The conservative man, we said, is one who isolates universal concepts and judgments from the transcending movement which he himself is. To this we can now add: man is conservative when he attributes the primacy to the universal essence and the species.

CHAPTER FOUR

Man As Original Reader

Contemporary thinkers are characterized by an increasing sensitivity to historicity and individuality. This has consequences for our idea of truth; individual history becomes a "place" where a truth comes to pass that cannot be brought to light by anyone else. The devaluation of immutable truth flows from this view. Because the many individuals are not interchangeable and therefore are inescapably marked by ownness, it also follows that truth can be pluriform without ceasing to be truth. Thus a kind of unity must be possible that is no longer the unity of a closed front.

Why is the ego an authentic source of truth? Summarizing the suggestions contained in the preceding pages, the answer is: because the unrepeatable ego is, precisely in its ownness, a meaning-giving project, a project which breaks open that which was fixed in order to give a new meaning to it in terms of the ego itself. If the ego decides not to do this, it does so at the expense of the transcendent movement which it is, at the expense of the dignity which pertains to it as a creative and free being. To renounce such giving of new meaning is not a matter of modesty but rather of pretension; it claims that the ending point has already been reached, for only then is there no need for further development. Only the ending point no longer belongs to history. One who pretends that he has already reached this point implicitly admits that he is no longer a historical being.

These ideas must still be developed. And the question how truth can be pluriform and in a process of development without ceasing to be truth must still be answered. In this and the following chapter we will illustrate both questions by means of a model, viz., the attitude of a reader with respect to a text.

The reason for choosing this model is the advantage it offers of bringing us into a clearly demonstrable situation and that it admirably fits in with man's historicity. For man is the heir of a centuries-old culture containing innumerable writings of great value. Moreover, a reader's attitude toward a text really offers a model for our understanding of the relationship between man and reality. In an analogously broadened sense we may call man a reader and reality a text.

This model has still another advantage. It offers a certain understanding of what theologians do, the nature of theological discussion and, therefore, also of the opposition between progressives and conservatives. For the theologian studies texts, viz., the Bible and dogmatic statements. That's why, as P. Schoonenberg remarks, the methods used by theology are in the first instance the methods of literary science.[1] It is a matter of fact that at all times theologians have been using one or the other form of hermeneutics. The distinction made by the ancient church between the "literal" and the "spiritual" senses of a text can serve as an example here. This use of hermeneutics means that the development of theology depends on, and is influenced by the development of philosophical hermeneutics, as is particularly evident from the history of the nineteenth century.

In what follows here, however, we will not speak of either Scripture or dogmatic statements, but the reason is not that Scripture is a sacred book, to which hermeneutics would not apply. Undoubtedly the Bible is a special book, but it is subject to hermeneutics; or rather, the explanation of the Bible, constitutes, together with classical philology and jurisprudence, the three streams that gave rise to modern hermeneutics. The reason why we wish to keep away from the Bible is that we desire to approach our topic in a philosophical way and therefore limit ourselves to philosophical texts.

---

[1] Schoonenberg, "Theologie werkt met methodes van de literaire wetenschap," *De Tijd,* Dec. 10, 1966.

In what sense, one can ask, does the philosopher have to concern himself with questions of reading texts? This kind of question will be asked by one who has grown up in the sphere of a conceptual philosophy. Such a philosophy pretends to speak directly about reality, for philosophy is an attempt to acquire knowledge of man, the world, the totality of being. One who philosophizes in such a way does not proceed in dialogue with other philosophers; these are mentioned only as being in favor of or against his own thought; and the latter is typically called a *thesis* which can be rigorously *proved*. The prevailing philosophy on the European continent today, however, lives in a different atmosphere. It is hardly inclined to posit any theses because it no longer assigns the primacy to the judging and positing intellect.[2] It prefers to point out rather than prove; it is able to see the value even of an idea which is badly or insufficiently proved or defended. Undoubtedly philosophy is an attempt to understand reality, but the limited understanding of which the individual is capable would almost be reduced to nothing if this individual did not constantly consult the great philosophers of the past. The heritage of these great thinkers is composed of certain writings of a philosophical nature. Thus the question of what he can and must do with those texts is of vital importance for a philosopher who wishes to enter into dialogue with the thinkers of the past.

1. The Starting Point

Let us assume that the texts to be read are very valuable. In that case it is not surprising that they are guarded as a precious heritage, to be counted among the best we have inherited from our ancestors. If the cultural asset contained in them is to be passed on to the coming generations, those texts must be carefully preserved. The term "preserved" is even too weak in some cases, for older texts often are no longer available in their original purity. Dating from before the invention of printing, they have come to us by way of manuscripts copied from older manuscripts. The manuscripts we possess contain texts transcribed many times, and the results of this are obvious. Transcribers make mistakes—some of which are like

---

[2] Cf. pp. 16 f.

those made by a typist or compositor—but these mistakes were not always noticed and corrected because there were no proofsheets. Besides, the owner of a manuscript often wrote his own remarks in the margin or in between the lines, thereby making it difficult for the next transcriber to determine whether or not those remarks were part of the text. In this way texts have been truncated, additions have crept in, and sentences dislocated.

Before we can preserve such texts, we must first "restore" them to their original condition. This is a laborious task, which is never completely successful. Besides, the situation is often even more complicated than indicated above. We may be dealing then with a text of which we cannot assume that it has ever been pure but later mutilated. For instance, the text may be one which a student wrote down to express the oral teachings of his master over the years. To what extent does such a text present us with a faithful representation of these teachings? Socrates himself did not write anything, but Plato, Aristotle and Xenophon tell us about his teachings. Their reports, however, are very divergent. Or there is question of a text describing the thought of a person which has remained alive for many years, spread through many circles and gone through a process of development. This is the case with Pythagoras. The texts we possess in such a case have arisen from that oral tradition; they are, as it were, a snapshot picturing a moment of a development which did not come to a standstill because the texts were written down. It is also possible that the original author revised his text, so that it reflects two different phases of his own development. Finally, the text can be the work of an editor who skilfully merged pre-existing texts written by others.

To "establish" a text, then, is a laborious task, to which many generations of scholars have devoted their lives. For this reason and because of the inner value of the text in which the heritage of our ancestors is laid down, the first requirement and the only correct approach is that we handle the text with care and reverence. People who think that, for instance, the text of Aristotle has finally been established with all possible purity rightly become indignant when the first comer makes Aristotle say something in a particular passage which he doesn't say there at all and which he says

perhaps nowhere. Reverence for the text is something demanded of
every reader. It is wrong to make a text say what it doesn't say. It
is also wrong to let the text speak in words which are not its own,
for terms and words imply the taking of certain positions.

May we do more, then, than simply print the integral text? It
stands to reason that we must establish what exactly the text says,
and this means of course that we should know the language it was
written in, Greek, Latin, Hebrew or whatever. The text perhaps
touches the same topic more than once; then we must ask, where?
how often? in what context? Besides, the text did not originate in
thin air but at a given moment of history; it shares in an era, makes
use of the terms then current, asks questions and formulates answers which were then in vogue. If the author of my text went
through a development, I must know the sequence in which his
works were written and where my text has its place in that
sequence.

In short, the reverence which we must show for the text demands that we accurately orientate ourselves to the text itself, to
this text, to be read according to its own character, as this text and
not that one.

2. *The Inadequacy of Fundamentalism*

Accordingly, to know what the text says we must reverently
address ourselves to the text itself. This may seem simple enough,
but in reality there is a serious problem here. There are two ways
of understanding that simple statement. Some people conceive it in
this way: reverently to address oneself to a text means that what
the text says can and must be established in absolute objectivity
and without any personal interference of the reader. The reader
must shut out his own subjectivity because otherwise he would
influence the text. Only when the reader himself is silent can the
text speak for itself. Others, however, say: while the reverence we
owe the text demands that the reader address himself to the text,
the text itself only speaks on the basis of a second consideration,
viz., the personal interest, expectations and prejudices of the reader. The reader is personally involved in his reading and it is only in

this involvement that the text can speak and announce a truth. One who—vainly—tries to eliminate this personal involvement will not do justice to the text.

This is the problem. Succinctly formulated it reads: is orientation to the text the total attitude in reference to the text or is this orientation only the first aspect of a total attitude containing two aspects?

Let us examine the problem somewhat more closely. If there is only one aspect—the first—I must limit myself to a pure and simple repetition of what is already in the text. I repeat it, I recover it from the past, take it up and carry it with me as an immutable jewel. All I do is repeat it and I must warn everyone to whom I pass it on always to repeat it without any change whatsoever. But in such a case isn't the text treated as if it were a material object, a precious family heirloom passed on from generation to generation? May one ascribe to the text the mode of being proper to a material object? And doesn't in such a case tradition become an oppressive burden?

On the other hand, if I defend that orientation to the text is only one aspect of an attitude composed of two aspects, I seem to encounter even greater difficulties. I am then forced, so it seems, to say more than is contained in the text. And by saying more than the text I seem to fail in the reverence owed to it.

The way of thinking which defends that orientation to the text itself constitutes the totality of our attitude with respect to it is called fundamentalism. This position is not entirely foreign to certain pursuers of philosophy. One has only to recall how Catholic thinkers used Thomas Aquinas; their approach is responsible for the fact that the genuine greatness of this philosopher is now largely discredited. More generally speaking, fundamentalism is the great danger to which every philosophical school of thought is exposed.

The question, now, is whether fundamentalism is really possible. It strikes us at once that the fundamentalist is not self-consistent. If he were, he would always have to repeat a Greek text in Greek, a Latin text in Latin, etc. Actually, however, he speaks English like everyone else in this country. Thus he must assume that he has at his disposal a perfect translation, one that adds nothing to the original and leaves nothing out. Obviously, such a translation is not possible. Every translator functions as an interpreter, he practices hermeneutics. And this at once introduces the second aspect.

Before we say more about this, let us first add that the fundamentalist is also inconsistent because he likes to quote. Any quotation cuts a fragment out of a larger whole. But who guarantees that this procedure is warranted? If the fundamentalist himself gives this guarantee, he is by the very fact personally involved in the text. If he really wished to be self-consistent, then he should every time repeat the entire text in its integrity. Even more important is the fact that it becomes impossible for the fundamentalist to accept that the text speaks to him, the reader, *in his history*, for he wishes to keep the text outside his own development, alleging that otherwise the text would evolve together with the development of his own ideas. This means that the reader in his development receives no support at all from the values represented by the text. But of what value is a text which is valueless for the reader's life-history? And why should such a text be reverently preserved for future generations who, likewise, will never be assisted by it?

These considerations also show the place to be assigned to the fundamentalist. The conservative, we said, is one who isolates universal concepts and judgments from the transcendent movement which he himself is. Now, the fundamentalist does this with respect to the universal meaning of a text. Hence "fundamentalist" is but another name for "conservative," but restricted to the conservative attitude with respect to texts.

We must now consider that reverence for the text demands precisely that we say more than the text has said to us, without, however, ascribing that "more" to the text itself. The demand that we show reverence for the text, then, is not tampered with. But we wish to point out that whoever doesn't have the courage to say more than the text is delinquent in reverence.

Let us pay attention to so-called *hapax legomena*, by which we mean here sayings or statements which occur only once in the text. Even before entering into details about this matter, one can imagine that addressing oneself to the text alone can be a source of embarrassment in connection with statements that are made only once. Similar, related or opposite statements can be juxtaposed, added to one another and compared, but which statement can I put side by side with one that is made only once? Solitary as it is, it seems to escape every effort of comparison. Should I say, therefore, that a solitary statement is unimportant? But that would be a weighty decision on my part, one which doesn't harmonize with my claim to address myself *solely* to the text. Moreover, it is not difficult to show that a solitary statement can occasionally be very important.

Let us give an example. Aristotle strenuously objected to a theory of Plato which he viewed as a fundamental mistake in the latter's entire philosophy, viz., the theory of participation in so-called Ideas. The clarity of his resistance leaves nothing to be desired. And yet just once Aristotle speaks of participation in a wholly positive way; in one passage of his *Metaphysics* (1030a 11-14) he seems to accept participation. This poses a problem to the reader. Should he disregard this one passage because it is the only one? But this would mean a lack of reverence for the text. And this lack of respect extends not only to that one passage but also to all those passages in which Aristotle objects to participation, for these, too, are now disputed. In other words, for one who disregards this one passage the entire metaphysics of Aristotle remains a closed book, even if he were to learn the text by heart. Is there, then, any solution for our problem?

According to Plato, participation is demanded wherever something is not fully identical with what it is. Participation, therefore, is needed for the things of the world; they may be called "beautiful" or "equal," but they are only partially beautiful or equal, so that they could also be called "non-beautiful" or "unequal." This means that they are beautiful or equal by participation. Aristotle, however, rejects this train of thought because he thinks that a substance, e.g., a man, is really identical with what he is. For a man is by definition a rational animal; man and rational animal are identical. Therefore, man is not a rational animal by participation.

But a second consideration follows. Man also has "accidental" qualities; for instance, he is tall and fair. Being tall and fair are not identical with being a man, for there are also short and brown-haired human beings. In this way Aristotle, despite all his fulminating against Plato's theory of participation, can serenely suggest in one passage that one is by participation what one is in an accidental way. The fact that he says it only once need not disturb us. There is no need to fear that he didn't really mean it or that that sentence was later added by a transcriber sympathetic to Plato's philosophy. For we realize that this conviction was implied in Aristotle's idea of substance.

What has happened here? Let us begin by pointing out that the preceding line of thought can nowhere be literally found in Aristotle. Plato, too, says nowhere that participation is required when something is not by full identity whatever it is. And Aristotle never states that participation must be rejected in the case of substance but can be retained with respect to accidents. What has happened here demonstrates that we cannot solve the problem if we limit ourselves to sheer reverence for the letter of the text. Such a limitation would fail to do justice to the text. The text itself demands that we say more than we find written in it; it demands interpretation.

3. The Necessity of Interpretation

The term "interpretation" is derived from the Latin *interpres*, and "hermeneutic" comes from the Greek *hermeneus*; both terms refer to one who translates, explains and makes us understand. A text demanding interpretation, then, is one that needs explanation to make us understand.

An interpreter is needed when people don't understand one another because they speak different languages. A text in a foreign language needs to be translated and, as we said before, any translation is an interpretation. There is, however, also a more profound obstacle to understanding than that offered by a language that is not known. This obstacle makes itself particularly felt when I decide to learn the foreign language in order to be no longer dependent on a translation. Only now that I can read that language the text appears to me as a foreign text with foreign terms and concepts, a text which refers to people, ideas and situations that are foreign to me, a text from a foreign world. But the text doesn't wish to be foreign to me; on the contrary, it wishes to reach me but doesn't reach me as long as it remains foreign to me.

This is precisely the cardinal point: the foreignness in which the text appears to me must be overcome. Otherwise the text *remains* foreign to me, it *tells me nothing* and therefore *cannot communicate any truth to me*. But who is able to take away the foreignness of the text for me? Certainly not the text itself, for it is precisely the text that is foreign to me. Therefore, only the reader is able to overcome this foreignness and to make the text say something. How does the reader attain this result? In principle the answer is that the reader must introduce the foreign text into his own world. It is from the reader's own world that the text derives the "plus" it reveals in interpretation. But this "answer in principle" still needs to be clarified and its implications must be disclosed. We will do this in the remainder of this chapter and in the one that follows.

The text owes its "plus" to the interpretation. To begin with, there is an increase of words. The interpreter adds more words; these are not arbitrary words but key-words of his interpretation. In the example given above—Aristotle's solitary statement of participation—the key-word is the term "identity" with the two qualifications "full" and "partial." If this word is left out, this interpretation fails; it does not succeed in making us understand Aristotle's statements about participation. At the beginning of this chapter we said that reverence for the text demands that we don't make the author say things which he never said. The interpreter doesn't do this; it is he who speaks in new words, not Aristotle. The interpreter must speak in new words, his own words, for only when he speaks in his own words does the text lose its foreignness for him, speak to him, disclose truth to him.

Let us now consider that "more" words implies also "more" truth, so that the interpretation adds a genuine "plus-value" to the text. What is a word? One who has been trained in a conceptual philosophy will answer: an arbitrary sign that could be replaced by another sign, at least if everyone would accept that other sign to express the same concept. In other words, a word is an arbitrary and replaceable sign expressing an idea that is already complete in itself. But in contemporary philosophy the word is rightly under-

stood in a different way. A thought is not first complete in itself
and then communicated to others through an arbitrary sign. Man's
thinking is an embodied thinking; that's why the word is an understanding which comes to itself in a concept, a concept that becomes
articulate and develops. In the above-mentioned example the use
of the word "identity" meant that genuine understanding was being
reached. What all this means must now be further detailed.

The text I read uses words, words that are strange to me before I
interpret them, but which were familiar and endowed with a
certain clarity when that text was originally written. We are speaking here of a valuable text which was rightly preserved for us over
the centuries. The text is valuable because it discloses truth about
the matter of which it speaks. This truth, then, came to pass in
words that were familiar at the time when the text was written
because they could be understood in the historical situation of that
time. But this means that the truth of the text is connected with
that historical situation; that's why this truth is "worded" only in a
limited and one-sided way. For reality is too rich for its truth to
come to pass exhaustively from a single standpoint. Any standpoint
is necessarily limited. The truth of the text is an incomplete truth;
one, moreover, that would not tell me anything and therefore
would be lost if I did not interpret it. By introducing the foreign
text into my own world and interpreting it, I protect its truth
against loss, but this protection is not simply a matter of preserving
the truth unchanged; it is the completion of the incomplete. This is
the sense in which the statement that the text demands interpretation must be understood.

In Section Four we will explore this idea further by a consideration of writing and the sense of historicity. First, however, let us
formulate a few conclusions which now impose themselves. The
statement that the reader gives a "plus" of truth to the text clarifies
our previous assertion that the ego, the individual man, is an
authentic source of truth. To this should be added that in a way of
thinking which ascribes the primacy to the individual—in a view
which considers the individual as a meaning-giving project—the
ego possesses an unrepeatable ownness, so that it is really different
from every other man and new with respect to him. The statement
that the ego is an authentic source of truth therefore means that

the ego brings about a really new truth. Because this applies to
every ego, the pluriformity of truth must be accepted. That this
does not imply a lapse into subjectivism and relativism we will
discuss in greater detail in the following chapter.

With respect to the model occupying our attention here—the
attitude of the reader to the text—it shows that there can be no
arbitrary subjectivism here just because the text itself demands
interpretation. The previously acquired truth could not even be
preserved but would be lost by alienation if there were no interpre-
ters; and the incomplete truth could not be brought to completion
without interpretation. Moreover, it should not be forgotten that
the interpreter brings the truth to greater completion because he
lives in a different situation than the writer of the text; this other
situation, however, is itself also a situation and for this reason his
words bring the truth to a greater completion but certainly not to
its final and definitive fullness. Even after my interpretation the
text continues to demand to be interpreted anew because otherwise
it would again become foreign to us. Awareness of this need should
put the interpreter on guard not to view his interpretation as
something fixed.

The absence of subjectivism also manifests itself when we consider that the interpreter must speak in new words, words that are
not arbitrary but chosen in such a way that they bring about a
more profound understanding of the text at issue. These words are
words spoken by the interpreter himself for they are not in the
text, but they are *commensurate* with the text; in this sense one
could say that they are *our* words, that is, of *me* and of the *text*
together.

4. The Written Word and Historicity

We are discussing the attitude of a reader toward a text. This
raises the question of the value to be attributed to a text, a written
word. The question is all the more urgent because in philosophical
tradition writings have been negatively appreciated most of the
time.

This negative evaluation can be found as early as Plato. Plato
preferred direct conversation. He viewed the written word as an

illegitimate brother of speech, a lifeless image of the living and animated reality of speaking. For the written word always says the same, it does not elaborate things further, while in a conversation or dialogue one can clarify, improve or defend one's ideas. Why should one make use of such an inferior instrument? The only reason can be to accumulate things to remember so that they can be used by the time one gets old and forgetful.[3]

The faultiness of this view shows itself when one considers the numerous cultural products which owe their existence to the written word. It goes without saying that the dialogue offers special opportunities beyond the written word, but this doesn't justify the conclusion that writing is merely an inferior substitute to be used when a dialogue is not possible. For Plato the written word is nothing but a memory crutch. This cannot be pushed to the limit, however, as is evident from the simple fact that one must at least remember that one has written something down and where. For there are people who put everything down in their memo-book and then forget to consult it.

The main accuser of the written word, however, is not Plato but Aristotle. He was the first thinker who devised a theory of the sign, a theory with which modern linguistics is still struggling today. The spoken word, says Aristotle, immediately renders the thought and reality, but the written word is a sign of the spoken word.[4] This means that the written word is only a sign of a sign; it is derivative, secondary sign, farther removed from reality than the living voice. It is to the living voice that the primacy belongs. This primacy of the living voice was emphasized again by Descartes' philosophy. He proposed the philosophy of the *cogito*, to which corresponds the living voice, for even as I think my own thinking, so I hear my own speaking, my own voice.

Hegel took up again Aristotle's idea: writings consist of "signs of signs." Husserl forms part of the transition to our time but remains in many respects bound to conceptual thinking; for him only the voice does not betray the solitary life of the transcendental ego. And J. Derrida[5] shows how much Rousseau's depreciation of the

---

[3] Plato, *Phaedrus*, 257c-277c.
[4] *De interpretatione*, ch. 1, 16a 3-6.
[5] *De la grammatologie*, Paris, 1967, and *L'écriture et la différence*, Paris, 1967.

written word has found its way into C. Lévi-Strauss, particularly the famous "writing lesson," which is Chapter Eighteen of his book TRISTES TROPIQUES. Writing is presented there as a means to exercise power and to exploit people and as a means of control through which the authorities subdue the citizens.

What could give us the right to go counter to such a long tradition and on what grounds could we still arrive at a positive appreciation of the written word? We could begin by pointing out that these authors themselves apparently do not agree with their own theory, tacitly contradict themselves and confess their theory only with their lips but not in practice. This is evident from the very fact that they have left a great many writings to posterity. It may suffice to refer here to Plato, who calls the written word a *pharmacon*. This word means poison and thus seems to indicate the harmful effects of the written word. But this same word primarily signifies a means, a means to restore health.[6]

Next, we could consider that the medieval thinkers who took over the Platonic-Aristotelian condemnation of the written word didn't hesitate to use strange expressions in spite of it. They speak of the *book* of nature, of God *writing* in the stars, and of the law of nature in which one can *read* God's will. Strangest of all, they used these expressions to indicate that we, human beings, can read these books only in a very defective way; the book of nature, for example, contains an inexhaustible mystery, only a part of which we can decipher. Wouldn't this viewpoint be a reflex of the high value which they attributed to one book, *the* book, the Bible? And didn't this appreciation of Scripture exercise influence on their appreciation of writings in general, even though it remains true that medieval man didn't manage to acknowledge this, even to himself?

The traditional rejection of the written word, however, only loses its force when we realize the prejudices on which it is based. Plato rejects the written word because there is no direct contact between writer and reader; his prejudice is that only the immediate presence to the other person results in truth. Aristotle views the written word as a derivative sign; only the spoken word is immediately present to the matter at issue. And Descartes gives preference

---

[6] Plato, *Phaedrus*, 230d 6.

to the living voice because the speaker hears himself speak; this is the prejudice of immediate presence to oneself.

The rejection, then, of the written word is based on a philosophy of immediate and momentary presence, that is, the philosophy of clear and distinct ideas as expressions of the fixed and immutable essence of things, the philosophy which rejects the individual and his history as extra-conceptual and empirical factors from which nothing good can come. Briefly put, it is a philosophy which withdraws the meaning of things from the dynamic movement that the giving of meaning and the coming-to-be of meaning is; it is afraid of the resistance offered by a text that never becomes fully transparent, and afraid also of interpretation which is always suspected of being different. The untrue elements contained in this philosophy have been criticized by Marx, Nietzsche, Husserl, Heidegger, Merleau-Ponty, Gadamer, Derrida and many others. What we are concerned with here is a way of thinking that does more justice to the non-momentary presence, to the so-called "empirical" aspect, to concealedness, the future and the hope of man as self-project and project of his world.

"Scripta manent" (writings remain), says an old saying. The manuscript and the book remain; first of all, as material objects, they continue to exist in time. But if I view a manuscript or book as a material object, I do not approach it precisely as the written word that is contained in it. The way the text continues to exist in time differs from that of the material object. Thus the meaning of the text can only be understood when one realizes the hermeneutic significance of typically human time, viz., historicity.

By way of orientation we could consider here that with respect to human time also there exist two opposing types of assertions. The first type is exemplified by "time heals all wounds"; the second by "time will tell" and "with time comes counsel." Time heals the wound inflicted on me; time will make me put myself at a distance from this painful moment, it will make me forget my pain. But the time which tells is not a time in which one forgets what one already knew, but a time in which one discovers the previously unknown.

But are these two series of statements really opposed to each other? Certainly, in time I forget many things, but does this mean that time must therefore be determined in terms of forgetting? Is time intended to make us forget? It may even be true that I *must* forget things because I would never achieve any genuine experience if I didn't forget anything at all of the things which I experience every day. But even this would mean that forgetting is not a final goal but orientated to man's growth. The meaning of time must be sought in growth and development. It is possible that I will forget my pain only after I have first discovered the truth about this pain. It is possible that my subconscious also only forgets and ceases to resist my consciousness after I have discovered the truth about my repressed desires.

The hermeneutic significance of time has been disclosed mainly by H. G. Gadamer, who bases himself on Heidegger. Since Heidegger, says Gadamer, we understand that time is not primarily an abyss that must be bridged. The temporal distance between the reader and the text is not something that must be overcome. On the contrary, it is important to recognize this temporal distance as a positive and productive possibility of interpretative understanding. Everyone is familiar with man's characteristic inability to understand contemporary works—e.g., contemporary art—with respect to which there is not yet any temporal distance. But according as the work loses its fashionable character, it can be enriched by productive time. This should not be taken to mean that it cannot be understood until it is dead enough to remain interesting only from a historical standpoint. But it means that the temporal distance allows the genuine meaning of the work to come forward, and it is this meaning, the truth disclosed by the work, that holds our interest.[7]

The core, then, of Gadamer's thought is this: time is not an abyss which separates and impedes understanding. This is precisely the point for which he bases himself on Heidegger, while paying attention only to the hermeneutic consequences of Heidegger's thought. He relies in particular on Heidegger's analysis of time, especially on the polarity of thrownness and project. Let us clarify this idea in our own way.

---

[7] Gadamer, *Wahrheit und Methode,* 2nd ed., Tübingen, 1965, pp. 275-283; see especially p. 281.

5. *Throwness and Project*

Why doesn't time constitute an abyss which separates and prevents understanding? To answer this question we must return to
the cardinal point of our considerations, viz., the statement that the
foreign character, the strangeness, in which the text appears to me
must be overcome. This statement needs further refinement with
respect to the terms "strangeness" and "me." For if the text were
absolutely strange to me, I would never be able to overcome its
strangeness. As a matter of fact, the strange text is familiar to me in
two ways, even before it loses its strangeness through interpretation.

Distinguishing the text from the book, we tacitly described the
text or the written word as bringing truth into language. But
independently of the text, I have already a measure of truth at my
disposal about the things spoken of in the text, for reality presents
itself immediately to me. The truth, then, brought by the text is
already to some extent my truth; I am already familiar with it. This
truth is familiar to *me* as a "projecting" being. Precisely because the
truth of the text is already somewhat familiar to me independently
of the text, I am able to introduce the text, unread and strange as it
still is, into my world, without thereby necessarily doing violence to
it or mutilating it.

This doesn't mean, of course that reading the text doesn't do me
or the truth much good. For the fact that I am able to overcome
the strangeness of the text means that this text receives a "plus" of
truth from my situation. And because I decide to read the text, my
superficial familiarity with the truth contained in it becomes more
profound, for the text's "plus" of truth arises from my interpretation.

My reading of the text, moreover, has a second effect on me.
This becomes evident from the second refinement that we must
make. We have already made the first refinement in the statement
that the text is strange to me. It defines the possibility of interpretation but it does not yet say anything about the question whether
time is, or is not, an abyss that separates. That's why we must now
make a second refinement.

The text is strange to me, we said, because it comes from a

strange world. What does this mean? Is the "world" of the text entirely different from the future "world" of the reader that came so many generations later? If this were true, then time would indeed be a separating abyss. But this is not the meaning of the assertion that the text is strange to me. First of all, because it would not at all be easy to indicate where the dividing line between those two worlds runs. Secondly—and this is more important—because the past and the future are dimensions of man as a historical being. Let us develop this point.

Man opens a future for himself because he is a project and opens new possibilities in his project. These possibilities, however, do not float around in a vacuum, as was thought by the philosophy of the pure *cogito*. All people think and they know that they think. A philosophy which only pays attention to this fact will be inclined to forget the individuality of man. Yet each man is an unrepeatable individual, and this means also that each man has his own starting point. The fact that man is characterized by historicity means that the new possibilities arising from his project are possibilities implied *in his thrownness*. The "projecting" man is preceded by that which makes all his projects both possible and limited. In his thrownness everything preceding him is offered to him as a condition for his project. The past is present to him, but—and this should be carefully noted—no longer in a momentary presence but in the typical presence of the past and in the mode of his thrownness. More simply expressed, every man stands in his own way in a tradition.

In the tradition of the reader, however, the text also plays a role. It is present in that tradition as a book that is being preserved, but this is not yet its presence precisely as a text. As a text the text is present in that tradition insofar as it has co-determined the tradition, in the sense that, without this text, the tradition would not be what it is. The text has been active in the tradition and that's why its influence did not leave the reader unaffected. This is also the ultimate reason why time is not an abyss, unless one means an abyss across which there is always and of necessity a bridge. One who is going to read a text has already been spoken to by the tradition and therefore by the text in question.

But if the text is already familiar to me, what remains of our previous assertion, to which we attached a capital importance, that the text arose in a foreign world, a strange world, whose strangeness I must overcome? The answer to this question is contained in what we have said above: the text is familiar to me in my *throwness*, but it is still strange to me as a *"projecting"* being. Undoubtedly, independently of the text, I already have a direct knowledge of the truth contained in it, but only in a superficial way, which has not yet been brought to a "plus" of truth through the reading of the text. That's why we said that the term "me" also needs to be differentiated. The strangeness of the text, which must be overcome in the interpretation, ultimately, therefore, is a strangeness which I carry in my own bosom; it lies in the fact that I am spoken to by a tradition which I have not yet taken up in the freedom of my project. For this reason the interpretation of a text is at the same time also a self-interpretation. This connection confirms that one's project of the world and one's self-project cannot be separated, even as also project and throwness constitute an "essentially unitary structure."[8]

Finally, the deficiency of the fundamentalist position should now be more evident. The fundamentalist would only be self-consistent if he were to repeat the total text—that is, all the works of its author—all the time in the original language. But he doesn't do this; he quotes and often he quotes in translation. We now realize that by doing this he adds a "plus" to the text—which is precisely what he doesn't wish to do. But he proves thereby that the reader cannot avoid giving a "plus" value to the text because he is a "projecting" and interpreting being. The fundamentalist is inconsistent because consistent fundamentalism is contradictory. One who wishes to be consistent must abandon the fundamentalist position and accept the implications flowing from this change in attitude.

---

[8] Heidegger, *Sein und Zeit*, p. 192.

CHAPTER FIVE

The Text As Norm
Of Reading

In the preceding chapter we have explained what is meant by interpretation and why interpretation is necessary and even inevitable. We intentionally limited ourselves there to a sketch of the essential aspects of contemporary hermeneutics. This restriction forced us to remain silent about the development from which contemporary hermeneutics has arisen; in particular, we said nothing about the hermeneutics of Schleiermacher and Dilthey. Our excuse for this omission is that we did not aim at completeness.

There is, however, another reason why we must now reflect upon the hermeneutics of these two philosophers. It is that in both cases this hermeneutics contains certain fascinating aspects. First of all, it falls short in a captivating way, a way that must be understood if one is to realize the scope of contemporary hermeneutics and the significance of certain key-concepts, such as "temporal distance" and "to understand." Moreover, their hermeneutics contains an element of truth that is sometimes jeopardized in contemporary hermeneutics, viz., the truth that the text remains the norm of my reading. In passing we have already referred to this point by saying that interpretation doesn't imply subjectivism or relativism. But this statement still needs to be further detailed.

There are also other questions that remain to be answered. For example, what does the interpretation establish? It gives a "plus" of value to the text and it enables me to overcome a strangeness which I carry in my own bosom, but how does this happen? And, finally, the following question also must be answered. If it is true that every reading is interpretative because of the unrepeatable character of the reader, does it remain possible to approach the text in a scientific fashion? For science doesn't move in the realm of individuality but precisely in the domain of the universally valid, the demonstrable and the verifiable. A theory of interpretation which cannot explain the scientific approach to the text must be wrong. For there obviously exists a textual science; it is called philology, and the important contributions to hermeneutics were made precisely by philologists and people with a strong philological background, such as Schleiermacher, Dilthey and Gadamer.

1. The Hermeneutics of Schleiermacher

Hermeneutics in one form or another has been in existence from the time that European man was interested in, on the one hand, Scripture, and on the other, classical literature. But this kind of hermeneutics was of a fragmentary nature and mainly composed of a large number of rules. Reading was viewed as something obvious, entailing no particular problems. Problems, so it was thought, arise only when reading comes to a halt because the reader encounters a difficult passage which he doesn't understand. When this happens, hermeneutics must offer him a principle with the aid of which he can understand the passage. For instance, a principle from which I can deduce that this passage isn't authentic and therefore doesn't belong in the text. Or, to give another example, let us assume that the reading comes to a halt in a passage permeated with an incorrect cosmology, one which no longer speaks to the reader. In this case hermeneutics can offer him the principle of allegory: the faulty cosmology is merely the wrapping of a spiritual truth. As soon as the allegorical significance is discovered, the reader is again on familiar terrain and can go on with his reading.[1]

This view of hermeneutics has been changed by Schleiermacher. It is not true, he says, that hermeneutics arises only from a non-understanding of the text; it arises from its misunderstanding. Man knows when he doesn't understand—namely, when his reading

---

[1] For a sketch of the old hermeneutics see Dilthey, *Die Entstehung der Hermeneutik*, vol. 5 of his *Gesammelte Schriften*, pp. 317-338. See also J. M. Robinson, *The New Hermeneutics*, New York, Harper and Row.

comes to a halt. That's why the old hermeneutic could be fragmentary. But man rarely knows what he misunderstands; it is possible to live for a long time in misunderstanding. This is the reason why the entire reading is threatened by misunderstanding. The new hermeneutics, then, must be universal; it must extend over the entire reading. To the old view, "I understand everything until I encounter a contradiction or nonsense," Schleiermacher opposed the view "that certain passages are difficult only because one also failed to understand the easy passages"; and he countered the idea "that understanding comes as a matter of course; one needs to be on guard only against misunderstanding," with the statement "that misunderstanding comes as a matter of course; but understanding must be willed and looked for."[2]

Schleiermacher had his reasons, of course, for being so vigilant with respect to misunderstanding and so diffident of understanding. In the earlier hermeneutics only difficult and incomprehensible passages were considered strange. But Schleiermacher was first is being sensitive to the strangeness which plays a role in every relationship of another human being to the ego. This strangeness exists in a conversation, a letter, but also in all writings and works others have left behind. This sensitivity is connected with another characteristic sensitivity, viz., for the individuality of each human being. One who experiences the unrepeatable ownness of every human being experiences at the same time that the other person is a stranger for the ego.

Schleiermacher managed to situate *this* strangeness very well. He was concerned with "a strangeness that must be understood," a "strangeness that must be changed into ownness"; no total strangeness, then, "for otherwise there would be no point of contact leading to understanding." But "if there was no strangeness at all between the one who speaks and the one who understands," hermeneutics would be entirely superfluous. Accordingly, hermeneutics stands in between the two poles of not-being-totally-strange and not-being-totally-familiar. The entire terrain between these two poles is covered by hermeneutics.[3]

---

[2] Schleiermacher, *Hermeneutik,* ed. by H. Kimmerle, Heidelberg, 1959, pp. 31, 79, 86.
[3] Schleiermacher, *op. cit.,* p. 128.

In this way not only the realm but also the function of hermeneutics is determined. If strangeness must be understood and in
this way changed into an ownness, the task of hermeneutics is to
analyze understanding. In Sections Three and Four we will criticize the two pillars of Schleiermacher's hermeneutics and show that
he incorrectly explains both strangeness and understanding. But
here we will limit ourselves to a statement of his view. What does
understanding involve according to Schleiermacher?

The strangeness which gives rises to hermeneutics is the
strangeness of the other human being. The text which I wish to
understand came forth from someone else and therefore is strange
to me. I will therefore understand the text only when I understand
this other human being, viz., the author. Here, in the psychological
interpretation, lies the novelty and the most original aspect of
Schleiermacher's view.

If understanding essentially goes out to the strangeness of the
other human being, then it isn't important that this other is an
author who died long ago. This situation isn't essentially different
from an immediate dialogue between living persons. Of course, in
the case of a text I must first enter into the past in which my
author wrote his work; I must gather the necessary historical
knowledge. But once I have acquired this knowledge, I have
become a contemporary of the writer. "Placing oneself on the same
level as the original reader," then, is the condition on which reading and colloquy cease to differ. As a condition that must be
fulfilled before understanding can begin, "placing oneself on the
same level as the original reader" differs from understanding itself.[4]

Once I have become a contemporary of the writer, I can come to
understand him in the same way as in a direct colloquy. As in a
colloquy I experience then how the other person handles the
language spoken by both of us in his own way and how he shapes
and develops in his own way the ideas that are current in our time.
I systematically pay attention to the things that are proper to him
and foreign to me. This attention bears fruit: suddenly I will
understand what is new in him; I have gained access to the

---

[4] Schleiermacher, *op. cit.*, p. 84.

creative process in him. Now that I have identified myself with him, the things proper to him are no longer foreign to me; I see how the text has arisen from his ownness. This is what understanding means; it is a "placing of oneself on the same level with the writer." Speaking and writing are constructive; understanding is a return to the point where speaking and writing originated and, therefore, a reconstruction (*Nachbildung*). Systematic attention is necessary, of course, but it is orientated to something else, viz., the sudden "placing of oneself on" the same level as the writer. For this reason understanding is not primarily "comparative" but "divinatory."[5]

2. The Hermeneutics of Dilthey

Dilthey repeats Schleiermacher's main ideas. For him also the strangeness which is the object of hermeneutics is "the strangeness of the other's life of the soul." He also considers all linguistic and historical attention to the text as "preparatory work that merely serves to place the modern reader in the situation of a reader from the time and the environment of the author."[6] And understanding ultimately is a "putting oneself into" a position in which one brings the writer's work back to the "experience" from which it arose; it is a "recapture of that experience" (*Nacherleben*). A well-known example is the following. Our time offers but few possibilities of religious experience. But if I read Luther's letters, I am confronted with a religious event, too explosive and overpowering to be experienced by modern man. Thus I cannot experience this event, "but I can recapture it."[7]

What is proper to Dilthey is that he puts understanding in opposition to explanation, which is characteristic of the method of the physical sciences. He argues that since Kant the physical sciences are methodically legitimated, but that the *Geisteswissenschaften*, the sciences of the mind, still lack a critical foundation. And his intention is to legitimate understanding as the method of

---

[5] Schleiermacher, *op. cit.*, pp. 123-126, passim.
[6] Dilthey, *Entwürfe zur Kritik der historischen Vernunft, Gesammelte Schriften*, vol. VII, p. 219.
[7] Dilthey, *op. cit.*, pp. 215-216.

the *Geisteswissenschaften*, so that the latter will not be less valid than the physical sciences.

Dilthey realizes, of course, that the *Geisteswissenschaften* speak in a different sense of experience than do the physical sciences. The latter disregard the particular and accidental in order to discover the universally valid. But the *Geisteswissenschaften* are concerned with the world that is "coming to pass" in its individualities. How can there be any universal validity there? Dilthey's answer is: "because I myself am a historical being; because the one who investigates history is the same as the one who makes history."[8] Heidegger and Gadamer could say the same, but they would not agree with what Dilthey implied with these words. Let us therefore explicitly state what Dilthey wishes to express.

He intends to say that in the *Geisteswissenschaften* subject and object possess the same nature and that for this reason the subject is able to overcome his own historical limitation. To do this, he must liberate himself from his particularity. According as man manages to detach himself from his own time, he attains an ever greater all-sided understanding. According as man overcomes his own relativity, *Geisteswissenschaft* reaches its objectivity. It stands to reason that it is difficult for man to overcome his particularity. This victory demands a process of growth in maturity, as is implied in Dilthey's typical remark that "old old age, the genius of under·standing, understands everything."[9]

3. Critique of the Presuppositions

The hermeneutics of Schleiermacher and Dilthey can be reduced to two directives, viz., "identification with the original reader" as the condition that must be fulfilled before understanding can arise, and "identification with the writer" as the essence of understanding. Both positions contain an element of truth, which will be considered in Section Five. Here we must consider that this hermeneutics fails to do justice to the true character of human understanding in its fullness. For this purpose we will criticize first the

---

[8] Dilthey, *op. cit.*, p. 278.
[9] *Op. cit.*, p. 225.

tacit presuppositions of their hermeneutics and in the following section we will criticize the positions themselves.

The primary presupposition of Schleiermacher and Dilthey is that the temporal distance between the text and the reader *must* be bridged. Reading and colloquy are not essentially different. They are different, of course, for the text dates from the past, but I neutralize the temporal distance by making myself a contemporary of the writer. Then I have done what I had to do; I have bridged time.

This general presupposition, however, is not tenable. Let us recall here the distinction between the reader in his thrownness and the reader as project. It certainly is true that the reader as a *"projecting"* being establishes a kind of bridge across time (cf. Section Five). But even in this respect one who emphasizes only this point fails to do justice to the full meaning of temporal distance. As we saw in the preceding chapter, it is not right to view temporal distance exclusively as something that must be neutralized. This distance is not a defect but a positive and productive possibility. Even more important is that the temporal distance is always already bridged for the reader *in his thrownness*. Time is not a separating abyss. For the reader stands in a tradition in which all the achievements of the past are present; tradition always has spoken to him already, and therefore also the text which was a codeterminant of this tradition.

Schleiermacher and Dilthey also self-consistently presuppose that the temporal distance *can* be bridged. How do they envision this bridge-building? Schleiermacher answers that the reader can put himself in the situation of the other person, first that of the contemporary reader and then that of the author, because he is sensitive to all other human beings. The basis of this sensitivity lies in this "that everyone carries within himself a minimum of everyone else."[10] In other words, Schleiermacher presuppose a fundamental community among all men, a community that is not purely formal but has a content which escapes historicity and which is not influenced by the differentiation of man into distinct individuals. Every man is

---

[10] Schleiermacher, *op. cit.*, p. 109.

for him all men. In a word, Schleiermacher remains within the sphere of thinking that ascribes the primacy to the universal human nature and the species.

Dilthey also proceeds from an image of man that ultimately is ahistorical. We understand the individuals, he says, because they are related to one another; the universally human is the foundation on which the individuals multiply.[11] Dilthey, moreover, is influenced by Hegel's idea that the opposition between individuality and universality, between finiteness and infinity must be overcome. He speaks, for example, of the "tragedy of the finite," and what he means is not that tragedy can occur in human life because of its finite nature, but that being-finite itself is tragic. Man "suffers from finiteness" and "tries to overcome it."[12] Dilthey's ideal must be seen in this context; the "understanding of everything" which only the old man can attain is an infinity that has overcome the finite.

What is the value of this presupposition? First of all, with respect to the reader in his thrownness, we may repeat that time is no separating abyss. The distance that must be bridged is present in man himself; it is the distance between man's thrownness and his project. Now, the possibility of bridging *this* distance lies in man's own essence; as a transcending movement man rises above everything *in* him that is pre-given *to* him.

But now the question returns in this form: how is it possible for man to transcend in a project the text as it is present to him in his thrownness? This question also has already been answered in the preceding chapter: he can do this because the truth of which the text speaks is to some extent accessible to him in a direct way and independently of the text. But this answer presupposes that reading the text is a coming-about-of-the-truth and not merely a "recapture" (*Nacherleben*) of an alien creativity. And this is a position that will be defended in the following section.

It is characteristic of Dilthey that he assigns a restricted domain to understanding, viz., the domain of the *Geisteswissenschaften*, in opposition to the physical sciences, which employ the explanatory method. His view expresses the presupposition that man's agreement can be separated from man's differences, so that man is not a

---

11 Dilthey, *op. cit.*, p. 213.
12 Dilthey, *op. cit.*, p. 244.

historical being down to his deepest core. But if man is essentially a transcending movement, he is historical to his inmost depth. And then understanding is no longer a *special method*; it is no longer even *any method at all*. Understanding *is* then man's projecting of himself and his world as the proper way in which man brings about his history. Understanding, says Heidegger, is the "fundamental mode" of man. Understanding in Dilthey's sense—as the counterpole of explaining—is only a "derivative" of the original understanding by which man is a human being.[13]

If Heidegger's view of man and his understanding is correct, one can easily see that becoming a contemporary of the original reader and the writer is impossible. One cannot possibly belong to the time to which one doesn't belong. And, therefore, *pure* reconstruction is also impossible. As we will see, in any reading there occurs something like a reconstruction, but this is not a pure reconstruction and, moreover, it functions at the service of productive understanding.

Finally, it does not make sense to speak of a "tragedy of finiteness" if this expression implies that I must renounce my individual ownness and my distinction from all others. One who posits such a view propagates a false ideal. It is not true that man must step out of history in order to survey history from a timeless position as a "disinterested spectator." Man stands in history as the collection of prejudices and possibilities which he is. That's why he mustn't act as if it were not true. On the contrary, he must bring himself along, as he is, to the work which he reads. Only this attitude is adapted to man's historicity.

4. Fundamental Critique

Becoming a contemporary of the original reader is only a precondition as far as Schleiermacher and Dilthey are concerned. The essence of interpretation, they hold, lies in the reconstruction of the creative process that occurred in the writer. Pure reconstruction, we said, is impossible, but could we perhaps maintain that the reader must come as close as possible to the disposition and situation of the writer? Isn't it commonplace to say that the writer

---

[13] Heidegger, *Sein und Zeit*, p. 143.

"means" this or that? And doesn't this mean that the discovery of the author's intentions is the essential task of our understanding?

Gadamer shows that this is not the case. He points out that understanding always has an object. When people understand each other, they have something to discuss; and they keep talking with one another until they agree very much about this "something." And when two people are said to get along very well, to understand each other very well, this expression means that they think more or less the same concerning all important matters; their views didn't clash. Understanding, then, has an object, it is orientated to some business; and people agree because all of them view that business pretty much the same way. Because the opinions don't clash, they don't draw attention; only the business at issue draws attention.

This situation changes, however, when we no longer understand each other and a misunderstanding arises. We then experience that we no longer communicate with one another by way of "some business." Does this mean that every possibility of communication has now disappeared? No, now that the business no longer holds my attention, the alien, incomprehensible, or even irritating opinion of the other person strikes my attention. I desire to understand that alien view. Perhaps I am wrong and the other person is right. That's why I return to the matter at issue to see whether perhaps the other's opinion can be defended. Let us assume that I don't succeed in this. Even then I don't abandon my desire for understanding. If the other's alien view cannot be understood at all *in terms of the matter itself*, I keep searching until I find an explanation of his strange view in his ethnic background, his education, his life-situation and his psyche as the result of all this. I offer a psychological interpretation.[14]

Schleiermacher's position should now be clear: his starting point is the situation in which spontaneous communication is cut off. He continues to adhere in this respect to the old hermeneutics, which was called upon to serve only when there was a failure of understanding. We may conclude that Schleiermacher and Dilthey erroneously saw as the very essence of understanding something that is only a derivative of it, viz., the understanding of a misunder-

---

[14] Gadamer, *Wahrheit und Methode*, pp. 168-169.

standing. Understanding, however, essentially is the understanding of the *matter* spoken of in the text; it is an event in which truth comes about. Thus the full meaning of the text ultimately depends neither on the original reader nor on the writer.

It may be useful to indicate more explicitly here, in reference to Schleiermacher and Dilthey, how the understanding of the text comes about. In doing this, we will keep the preceding analysis in mind, but we will differentiate it by starting from the position that the reading aims primarily at the matter contained in the text.

As has been pointed out, I am always to some extent familiar with the text because the text has spoken to me in my thrownness, and with the matter spoken of in the text because, as project, I am in contact with this matter already and independently of the text. That's why I can recognize the matter spoken of in the text, even though it appears there in an alien form. This is my primary experience: there is a recognized truth which I experience none-theless as *alien* because I would certainly have expressed it *differently*. What is involved here is an experience and not a sober intellectual insight. I am struck by the otherness of a familiar truth which, to the extent that this truth is different, I do not at once understand and which therefore makes me uneasy, for man re-mains at ease only when everything goes according to his expecta-tions. That's why from the very first moment I am fully involved in my reading. It is possible for me, of course, to deny the unrest implied in this experience, for I can deny everything that threatens to disturb my peace. But in that case I refuse to accept the experience which the text gives me. In this refusal I make myself a simple spectator who isn't involved, a spectator who looks at the text from an extra-temporal standpoint. I thereby make my histori-city as inoperative as possible. Under such circumstances the truth which in such conditions I can still gain from the text will inevi-tably be reduced.

Accepting the strangeness of the recognized truth, however, doesn't mean that I am resigned to it; I now have the task of reconciling this strangeness with the truth that was already familiar to me and on the basis of which I was able to recognize truth in the text. This task has two sides; it is concerned with the otherness and the familiarity of the truth of the text. I must realize in what respect and why the truth of the text is different and, at the same time, what the basis is of my familiarity.

As always when communication is broken, so also in this case where communication is only partial, *I return to the matter itself.* Now that I have been roused from my slumbers and take a fresh look at the matter, it can become evident to me that I never before studied it carefully because I relied on a pre-judice which cannot stand scrutiny. In this case I lose a putative truth and this brings me closer to the truth.

The preceding sketch isolates a single aspect from the total event. The total event is much broader. For by way of tradition the text has always spoken to me even before I read it; and independently of the text I am also already somewhat familiar with the matter of which it speaks. That's why I have a large number of pre-judices about this matter, and not all of these pre-judices can be unreliable. Some are reliable and some unreliable. But I don't know which ones are right and which ones wrong, for pre-judices are not judgments made with full consciousness. On the basis of the complex of my pre-judices, then, I expect that the text will speak in this or that way. But precisely in this expectation the text contradicts me; it speaks differently. In this way the otherness of the text upsets the entire complex of my pre-judices, causing in me the uneasiness which is the primary hermeneutic experience we have mentioned above.

From this uneasiness *I then return to the matter,* with the firm intention of taking a good look at it. In this inquiry I attain truth about the matter. This truth will contradict some of my pre-judices, so that I reject them, and confirm others, so that they now reach the rank of judgments; others, again, will be left untouched because the matter was unable to throw any light on them. Thus I don't merely attain truth about the matter, but I also begin to understand from which standpoint I myself view this truth. Reading the text again, I am better equipped than before; I am now able to recognize from which standpoint, in opposition to my own, the text has approached one and the same truth.

I also begin to notice the pre-judices underlying the text, and some of these I see as wrong. This means that now I am able to

criticize the text, that is, to strip it of untruth. Others of the text's
pre-judices are not wrong, but I realize that they are connected
with the past situation from which the text speaks to me. This
means that I am able to speak the truth of the text in my own way,
in a new way. In this way I transcend the strangeness of the text, I
prevent its truth from being lost, and I "preserve" this truth in the
only way a non-material entity can be preserved, viz., by increasing
it and bringing it to greater completion. In addition, I must assume
that there is a third group of pre-judices; they are pre-judices
common to the text and myself; these are not brought to light by
my reading. Regarding this group, which doesn't enter my
awareness, I may not exclude the possibility that a later reader will
find himself compelled to translate those pre-judices also into the
new words of a later era.

Finally, it can happen that my communication with the author
regarding the matter at issue remains unfruitful; the text remains
foreign to me and unintelligible. In such a case my deep-rooted
tendency toward intelligibility will lead me toward a psychological
analysis of the author.

5. The Truth of the Reconstruction

To discover the element of truth present in the hermeneutics of
Schleiermacher and Dilthey, we must first of all keep in mind the
absolute opposition between fundamentalism and hermeneutics.
Fundamentalism rejects every intervention of the reader, but such
an intervention is accepted in hermeneutics, whether that of
Schleiermacher and Dilthey or our own. Fundamentalism wants
the text itself and nothing but the text; hermeneutics claims that
the text cannot be as a text without the reader.

Fundamentalism, we saw, is an impossible project. But the existence of a project cannot be explained by saying that it is impossible. Fundamentalism arose because people wished to attain a
certain goal and didn't realize that this goal couldn't be reached in
that way. Fundamentalism is impossible because it desires "nothing
but the text," for even the most innocent reading, any quotation
and certainly any translation, adds a "plus" to the text. But the
fundamentalist aims at "the text itself"; and in this he is right. The

reader must orientate himself to the text; he must read it according
to its own nature, as this and not any other text. A reader to whom
several, quite different texts say exactly the same disregards everyone of these texts. He doesn't interpret but indulges in reading
something into it that is not there; what he says is not an interpretation but a misinterpretation.

Strange as it seems, the fundamentalist cannot accept any difference between interpretation and misinterpretation, for the simple
reason that any "plus" is more than he can swallow. But this very
position shows that fundamentalism cannot do justice to what it
rightly wishes to attain. The legitimate goal of fundamentalism can
only be attained by means of hermeneutics; for only when the
"plus" of the reader is accepted is it possible to make a distinction
between a justified "plus" and an unjustified "too much."

This conclusion can be presented even more stringently. The
fundamentalist poses as the defender of objectivity without any
subjective addition. But it has now become evident that it is
impossible for the fundamentalist to distinguish between a faithful
and a perverted reading. Thus, in the realm of reading his desire
for objectivity means that the question of truth can no longer be
raised. Because it makes use of objectivity as criterion in a realm
where this criterion doesn't belong, fundamentalism is objectivistic.

Let us add at once that reading something into a text disregards
the text and therefore is a kind of subjectivism. Now, subjectivism
implies arbitrariness and control of truth by private interests. Thus
it follows that a genuine interpretation—one that lets itself be
guided by the text—escapes the dilemma of either objectivism or
subjectivism. The interpretation doesn't claim to be objective but
only to have listened to the text itself. That's why it attains the
truth.

Fundamentalism must surrender its task to hermeneutics, but to
which hermeneutics? Can the rightful desire of fundamentalism be
satisfied within the hermeneutics of reconstruction? We must continue, of course, to hold fast to the conviction that reconstruction is
not the whole essence of understanding, for the latter is productive. We will only have recourse to the psychological interpretation
which tries to reconstruct the author's creative process when all

efforts to understand the strange text through the matter itself have failed. But, according to Schleiermacher and Dilthey, psychological understanding is possible only on the basis of a long and systematic attention to what is proper to the text and strange to me. Now, this demand satisfies the desire of fundamentalism. In this respect, then, the hermeneutics of reconstruction is true.

The purpose of systematic attention to what is proper to the text should be obvious. The fruitfulness of the interpretation is based on the hermeneutic experience, the experience of the alien character of a truth that is, nonetheless, recognized. This experience, we said, may not be weakened by a refusal of the restlessness which it evokes. I may not withdraw to an extra-temporal position, but I must bring my very ownness into play. On the other hand, a second condition must also be fulfilled. The fruitfulness of the hermeneutic experience depends also on the extent to which I am really confronted by the ownness of the text. For it is precisely in its ownness that the truth of the text is different from what I expected. Accordingly, my confrontation with the otherness of the text, together with the contribution of my ownness, determines the power of the hermeneutic experience. That's why this confrontation is decisive for the fruitfulness of that experience and for the truth of my interpretation.

Let us summarize the results achieved. Reading gives a "plus" of truth to the text. Therefore, every reader, this individual human being in his newness and originality, is an authentic source of truth. Interpretation is pluriform, as manifold as there are authentic readers. Hence a pluriformity of truth must be accepted. Nevertheless, this doesn't mean falling into relativism or subjectivism; for interpretation differs from reading something into a text; the interpretation is governed by the text itself as its norm, while reading something into a text disregards this text. Now, it is not necessary that truth be immutably and exactly the same for all human beings; what is necessary, however, is that truth satisfy the norm.

The statement that truth must satisfy the norm has, of course, a bearing on the nature of pluriformity. This should be clear from our model, the reading of a text. There is a pluriformity of interpretation, but the many different interpretations are all governed by the same text as their norm. Yet the pluriformity is genuine because every authentic reader is a new human being having an original standpoint, capable of opening up tradition in a new way toward a new future. His interpretation, therefore, brings about a truth which cannot be brought to light by anyone else.

6. The Role of Philology

If it is true that the reading is interpretative because of the unrepeatable individuality of the reader, does a scientific approach to the text remain possible? We asked this question at the beginning of this chapter, but the answer has not yet been given. In a way, the answer is very simple: philology, which is a science of the text, does exist; therefore, such a science is possible. More properly formulated, then, the question is not whether this science is possible, but how a place can be assigned to it in our hermeneutics.

Let us take up again the thread of our considerations in the preceding section; in other words, we start again from the absolute opposition between fundamentalism and hermeneutics, *tout court*, including that of Schleiermacher and Dilthey. Philology then lies on the side of hermeneutics, for fundamentalism is an impossible project while philology is, like any science, a meaningful and fruitful human attitude. Philology accepts the "plus" of reading, for it orders, compares and studies the statements made in the text.

But with which aspect of hermeneutics should philology be connected? The full scope of hermeneutics is that the reader introduces the truth of the text into his ownness in order to overcome its strangeness. This process, we said, has two aspects: the individual ownness of the reader is put into play and the reader is confronted with the ownness of the text. Now the contribution of the reader's individual ownness cannot primarily be the aim of philology because philology is a science and therefore aims at universal validity. This means, then, that philology is orientated to the other aspect. It intends systematically to establish the ownness of the test.

Accordingly, philology stands on the side of the hermeneutics of reconstruction. It tries to become contemporary with the original reader and to discover the writer's intention. It is, therefore, the

systematic attempt to prevent the reader from falling into the
subjectivism of reading something into the text.

Reconstruction, however, we saw, is not the full scope of hermeneutics; in a similar way the philological attitude is not the full
scope of the attitude which the reader should take in reference to a
text. Philology, therefore, cannot speak the decisive word about the
meaning of a text. Only the reader himself can do this as one who
brings into play both the ownness of the text and the ownness
characterizing himself as this ego. Because the philologist represses
his ownness and tries to assume an extra-temporal position, his
interpretation remains insufficient. It is important that he realize
this; and the non-philologist on his side should realize that the
philologist has freely opted for a scientific approach.

Because the philological interpretation is insufficient, it remains a
partial interpretation; only the commensurate interpretation can
express all the data of the text in a single translation of their
meaning. This fact finds expression in the preference which philologists show for calling their studies "commentaries." I'd like to
define the commentary as the interpretation which establishes the
text's ownness in order to prevent reading things into it that are not
there, but which remains insufficient because it artificially eliminates the commentator's own standpoint.

CHAPTER SIX

Alienation And Ownness

The problem of alienation, which we will now discuss, must serve primarily to clarify the perspective on man within which all our discussions take place. In particular it must serve to clarify the position of the conservative man. Man, we said, has two possibilities; he is progressive as a transcending movement, and he is conservative to the extent that he isolates universal concepts and judgments from the transcending movement which he himself is. We can now no longer evade the question of how these two possibilities of man are related to each other.

In addition, we have pointed out that one who assigns the primacy to the individual runs into difficulties with respect to the relationship of the ego with other people. If the ego is a meaning-giving project, then the ego, so it seems, can meet the other person only as one "projected" by his project. But, in this case, doesn't the ego of necessity fail to reach the other person as he is in himself? And doesn't it become entangled in an absolute solitariness, in the same way as Husserl's transcendental ego or Heidegger's authentic man? The approach to these problems demands the development of a theory of alienation or estrangement.

And, finally, in the next chapter it will become evident that the theme of secularization can only be understood on the basis of the idea of alienation.

1. Is Earthly Life an Estrangement?

In Augustine one can find an idea which our non-Christian contemporaries reject without any qualification and which stumps the contemporary Christian also, even though he recognizes this idea as one handed down to him by tradition, viz., the idea that life on earth is an alienation, that man is a stranger on earth.[1] What exactly does Augustine say, which sources influenced him and what is the picture of man from which he proceeds?

Augustine tells us that we human beings are pilgrims; that's why we cannot be really happy on earth. We should desire nothing more than to see the end of our unhappy situation. We must long for our home, our fatherland, heaven; we must go to heaven, for only there can we be happy. If we were to be pleased with our earthly life, we would no longer desire to see this life ended. But we would then become estranged from our home. For this reason we may not enjoy this world although we must make use of it.[2]

For Augustine, then, estrangement is alienation from our heavenly home and from happiness; man is struck by this estrangement as soon as he goes counter to his condition as a wayfarer by enjoying life instead of merely making use of it. Augustine did not say that earthly life is an alienation, but what he did say produced the same effect because earthly life cannot be led without a measure of happiness. In other words, the fact that we can make use of the world fills us with joy. Augustine's own autobiography shows that he himself also experienced this. The reason why he does not say that earthly life is an alienation, *tout court*, is that he has already made a Christian correction on his sources.

One of these sources is the Jewish writer Philo. He says that all people have come from a heavenly fatherland. But when they forget this, they act as if they are settlers, people who have left their country for ever. These are sinful people, they establish themselves on the earth as if it were their homeland. The wise man, on the contrary, is not a settler but a pilgrim. The earth is not his fatherland; he merely is there on a journey. Philo, however,

---

[1] Cf. R. A. Markus, "Alienatio. Philosophy and Eschatology in the Development of an Augustinian Idea," *Studia patristica*, vol. IX (1966), pp. 431-450.

[2] Augustine, *De doctrina christiana*, I, 4, 4.

adds an idea which we no longer find in Augustine, viz., the idea that because the wise man does not establish himself on earth, he estranges himself from his body, for the body is valued as it ought to be only when one says: it is alien to me, it does not belong to me.[3]

Philo's addition makes us recognize the picture of man underlying his ideas. He repeats the characteristic features of Plato's anthropology. For Plato man is, strictly speaking, a soul which pre-existed before it became connected with a body; that's why he values the body in a negative way. And this negative appreciation is extended to the world, for we are in the world by way of our body. Man must flee the world; by fleeing it, he becomes like unto God.

The same image of man is also found in the neo-Platonism of Plotinus. He is convinced that the soul can only return to God if man "remains a stranger to his body."[4] More strongly even than Plato, Plotinus states that the soul was originally one with God—so much even that it was "a part" of God.[5] His problem is precisely how the soul could ever forget God its Father, despite the fact that it is a part of God. In a word, within this Platonic anthropology man is, strictly speaking, a divine soul, and that's why earthly life, in which the soul is connected with a body, is really an estrangement.

Augustine never managed to detach himself from this anthropology although he made certain corrections in it. This failure manifests itself, for example, in the fact that his theory of human emotions is not self-consistent. He sometimes even contradicts himself. For instance, he argues that man has his emotions in common with animals and that's why we must subjugate them. For otherwise they break loose and carry us away toward pernicious pleasures. But if we subject them, they become tame and we can live in peace with them. Immediately after saying that our emotions are at best comparable to tame sheep, he adds inconsistently, "for the movements of our soul are not foreign to us."[6]

The most striking characteristic of Plato's anthropology, however,

---

[3] Philo, *De confusione linguarum*, XVII, 75-82.
[4] Plotinus, *Enneades*, V, 1, 10 line 27.
[5] Plotinus, *op. cit.*, V, 1, 1, line 2.
[6] Augustine, *De Genesi contra Manichaeos*, I, 20, 31.

is the pre-existence of the soul. And this pre-existence constitutes the unquestionable background of the pilgrim concept. For whether man is evil and behaves as a settler or wise and behaves as a pilgrim, in either case he existed already before he faced the earthly choice of becoming a settler or a pilgrim. He was already there; that is, he was with God, in heaven, in the fatherland to which he must return.

It is very important to realize how easily a Christian will take over this Platonic idea. To return to Augustine, for some time he accepted the pre-existence of the soul, but later he explicitly rejected this view. Nevertheless, in our opinion, he continued to think in this perspective. The reason why he did this is that one is readily inclined to explain creation in line with this Platonic thought. It seems so "obvious" to think that man, who is created by God, was with God before he was created in time. And God's "eternal love" of man seems to point to His love for us before we originated in time.

This is, of course, a faulty explanation of creation. It speaks of a "before" creation, but time and the distinction between "before" and "after" arose only through creation. Besides, it detracts from God's creative power because creation in the strict sense does not presuppose anything[7] and is total causality. But once creation is explained in such a faulty way, one easily takes over the Platonic view of man, one is inclined to consider the body and the whole of earthly life as an estrangement, and embarrassed by the Genesis statement that "God saw that it was good."

One consequence must still be pointed out explicitly. If we deny that earthly life as such is an estrangement, we also reject the idea that the human soul ever existed as a pure and divine spirit before it entered the body. Earthly man is not an "intermediary stage" between a pure starting point and a pure terminus. Man is on the road, we think, to a pure terminus, but he doesn't have a pure starting point.

The Platonic-Augustinian wayfarer's theory has had a long life among the preachers of Christianity. But on the level of explicit reflection its influence has steadily diminished. Sociologically

---

[7] Thomas Aquinas, De potentia, 3, 5, ad 2.

speaking, this Christian version of Platonism belongs to the era of
the persecuted Church; it lost power when Christianity became
socially respectable. Theologically it was weakened by the struggle
against Manichaeism, which ascribed the body to a separate principle of evil. Philosophically it lost strength because thinkers acquired a better understanding of man's unity and the true meaning
of creation. Thomas Aquinas especially was of great importance in
this respect. A symptom of the diminishing importance of this
Platonic theory is that as early as Ambrose a correction was made
on Plato's flight from the world. The soul which is on the road to
perfection, says Ambrose, tends to the divine and flies from earthly
matter. But this flight doesn't mean that it leaves the earth, but
that it practices justice and sobriety on earth and renounces vice.[8]

As a consequence of all these influences the idea of estrangement
hardly continued to make itself felt in theoretical reflection after
Augustine. When many centuries later it emerged again, this happened in a new form and in connection with a new historical
situation. Estrangement then became a phenomenon within the
world and, in particular, an element of man's historicity.

2. *The French Revolution and Estrangement*

In 1798 Kant asked himself what the prospects are for the moral
future of mankind. Some people, he pointed out, say that the
human race will go from bad to worse; but this is impossible, for
otherwise mankind would eliminate itself. Must we say, then, that
there is continuous progress? But how could one show that there is
such progress? Or does mankind go sometimes forward and then
again backward, so that good and evil neutralize each other?

These questions, says Kant, cannot be solved by an immediate
appeal to experience. Even if mankind went forward for a long
time, no one would know whether it was not on the verge of going
backward; reversely, if mankind went backward, it could perhaps
turn again to the good. God, of course, knows the answer, but we
aren't God. And this means that we must, nonetheless, answer the
question by way of experience. There must be an experience in the
human race which clearly shows that man possesses a capacity for

---

[8] Ambrose, *De Isaac vel anima*, 2, 3–3, 6.

the ever-better, an experience which is not the cause of progress but the sign of man's capacity for the better.

Now, such a sign has just been made in history by the revolution which has taken place in a different nation but which everywhere, even in our own country, has been greeted enthusiastically. "For such a phenomenon in the history of mankind cannot be forgotten because it has disclosed in human nature a capacity for the better which no politician has ever been able to lay bare in the preceding course of history." Those who claim that a restoration will follow upon the revolution may be right, but this doesn't mean that the revolution can be undone: "this event is too great," it will continue to influence mankind. It also gives us a better understanding of the past. We understand that mankind has always been developing toward a better condition.[9]

The idea of progress was born from the French Revolution. Man develops toward self-consciousness and freedom, as Hegel says. But this implies that man is not yet what he "is," he must still realize himself as man.

What about the present situation? It is far from ideal; only a beginning has as yet been made. Our time is evil, sinful and imperfect. Goethe, Fichte, Herder, Novalis, all prominent representatives of German humanism, emphasized this, as was done also by the thinkers who after Hegel exercised critique on the situation of their time and spoke of a "war against the German conditions" (Marx).

If man is always on the way toward something better, how is he able to live in a world that is out of harmony with his ability? Only "dialectics" can answer this question; that is, the actual situation is an estrangement of man's essence.[10] The philosophy of alienation of both Hegel and Marx must be seen against this background.

F. Grégoire explains Hegel's fundamental idea in the following way. Hegel starts from man's limitation and finiteness, but how does man experience this limit? Faced with the boundless diversity and constant change of nature, man becomes confused. For things and

---

[9] Kant, *Der Streit der Fakultäten*, II, 7; in the Wissenschaftliche Buchgesellschaft ed. of his works, Darmstadt, 1968, vol. 9, p. 361.

[10] H. Popitz, *Der entfremdete Mensch*, Darmstadt, 1967, p. 30.

events impress him as strange and hostile. This feeling does not become weaker when man faces his fellowman and especially not when he reflects upon history and recalls the perplexing succession of civilizations choking one another to death, and of religions and customs such that one cannot understand that they could ever have existed or continue to exist. Thus man experiences reality as separated from him, and himself as separated from reality. The strange and hostile character of reality evokes a feeling of separation, division and estrangement. Man doesn't recognize himself in reality, he feels lost; reality doesn't have a human shape.

Man, however, can become reconciled with the world, his fellowman and himself. But he cannot do this by a romantic "longing," which leaves the finite as it is in order to orientate itself directly to the Absolute. For then the finite remains strange and hostile, so that man is not at home with himself. On the contrary, man must transcend finiteness by discovering the human element already present in reality or by giving a human form to reality, as he does in his work. Then man will recover himself and "be with himself." This is the reconciliation in which the spirit—for Hegel's man is reason (Vernunft)—will arrive at a perfect harmony with the whole of reality, and in it all finiteness and opposition will be overcome.[11]

From this core Hegel proceeded to develop a philosophy of self-realization. His starting point was that man is free by nature. But this is merely a natural freedom, a freedom that is his lot because that's the way he is; in other words, a freedom with which he has not yet anything to do. For this reason man must rise above his natural immediacy toward the level of a more conscious and more self-conscious encounter with himself, his fellowman and the world. But when he tries this, he experiences what is alien to him and restricts him; for example, he encounters the state which subjects him to its laws. Subjected to the alien, he is dependent and not free, a situation that is necessary if he is to become free in a human way. But it also means that self-realization doesn't stop at this level. Man must overcome the alien character of what he encounters; he realizes, for example, that his true essence needs the supra-individual reality which the state is. By uniting the alien

---

[11] F. Grégoire, Etudes hégeliennes, Louvain, 1958, pp. 1-9.

with himself, he transcends his unfreedom and he authentically realizes himself as the man he was already by nature.

If man is a self-realizing being, then he must be a being characterized by historicity. In this way estrangement is now a component of self-realization and therfore also of historicity.

But Hegel's concept of estrangement has two aspects. Estrangement, *tout court*, is necessary, for otherwise self-consciousness and freedom don't transcend the natural level. "Self-consciousness is something, has any reality, only insofar as it becomes estranged from itself."[12] This alienation could be called the positive component of self-realization. But in addition to this necessary alienation Hegel knows estrangements that aren't necessary and should be avoided but which, whenever they occur, exercise a negative function within man's self-realization. Such an estrangement is the romantic "longing" (*Sehnsucht*), which leaves that which is strange as it is. And because man must put his stamp on reality through his work, those who wish to be "clean souls" alienate themselves, that is, they abstain from acting and working for fear of getting dirty hands. Faith also is such an estrangement, but the situation of faith is rather complex.

By faith Hegel means a form-of-religion which has not yet come to itself, but at the same time he conceives religion as itself not yet the genuine reconciliation of all opposites; for this reconciliation will occur only in absolute knowledge. The imperfection of faith consists in the fact that it is an attitude which accepts two worlds. Faith incorrectly thinks that this world is not truly intelligible and therefore assumes a negative attitude toward it; it is a "flight from the real world."[13] It takes refuge in a "world to come" (*Jenseits*), a heaven, assigning to this heaven all the intelligibility which it denies this world.

What is the foundation of this misunderstanding? To the Spirit belong both the unrest of self-movement and the rest and satisfaction of being at home. But faith has disconnected these two elements.[14] That's why faith passes by the world, for the latter

---

12 Hegel, *Phänomenologie des Geistes,* Glockner ed., p. 377.
13 Hegel, *op. cit.,* p. 376.
14 Hegel, *op. cit.,* p. 407.

necessarily remains not-understood, strange and finite. And faith also passes by self-movement and self-realization, for it does not direct itself to the "self" but to an infinite content that remains alien to the "self," a God who spatially and temporally is far from us.

Now, faith undoubtedly has its place in the gallery of forms in which the Spirit ascends to his freedom. Insofar as faith has no real object—for heaven is not real but only the result of alienation—it is a preparation for the absolute knowledge which has no longer any object because the "self" has itself as its object. But since the Illumination and since Hegel have shown the way to the reconciliation of all opposites, one irrevocably becomes estranged from himself if one holds on to faith as if it were no preparation.

The necessary estrangement lies, according to Hegel, mainly in the power struggle between individuals and groups of individuals. The alienation of people from one another can only be transcended if every man recognizes that other people are human beings just like him. A necessary stage preceding this mutual recognition, then, is the situation of one-sided recognition, and this is a situation of necessary estrangement. The one-sided recognition is marked with the sign of the master-slave relationship. Let us see whereto the situation of the "self-estranged spirit" leads.

Man in his "natural immediacy" sees the other self as a threat to himself. He denies the other self and this means that he should kill him. But from the dead one cannot expect any recognition; that's why the struggle to death between men terminates in the surrender of the one to the other; the slave recognizes his master. But this is a forced and one-sided recognition. For this reason the situation of the slave who recognizes the self-consciousness of his master cannot be the end. Hegel shows how the relationship turns into its opposite. Because the master enjoys things and by enjoying them consumes them, he becomes dependent on products which are created by the work of the slave and bear his seal. The slave arrives at self-consciousness through his labor. His work makes him self-conscious, but this has been made possible by the fact that the slave, before surrendering to the master, endured the fear of death;

"everything fixed in him was shaken" and he gave up his "immediacy."[15]

The power struggle between groups of people also results in such a dialectical turning-over in which opposites lose their oppositional character. Hegel starts here with the power of the state, by which he means the established order. The base consciousness refuses to obey the state, but the noble consciousness recognizes the established order and puts it above one's private interests. This is "the heroism of service," by which Hegel means the era of feudalism and the "proud vassal" who effaces himself. The vassal speaks the language of the council in which he expresses the general sentiment of the people to the sovereign. But this council is ambiguous, for while expressing the general sentiment, it conceals its own opinion. That's why feudalism ends in an era of absolute monarchy; for even one's own opinion has to be sacrificed.

The language of the council, says Hegel, has to become totally language, that is, an exteriorization which discards even one's own opinion. This happens in "the heroism of flattery," which is the point at which the sovereign becomes an absolute monarch. But at this very moment the situation changes into its opposite. Because the power of the state owes its reality and its sustenance to the total sacrifice made by the noble consciousness, the power of the state has really been passed on to this consciousness. In this way the noble consciousness attains what the base consciousness wished to attain. The general power has gone to the slave. Henceforth this power exists as wealth.

Wealth shares its riches. But in its immediacy wealth does not share as an altruistic nature but as a being which, even while giving, holds fast to itself. Because it keeps the other person alive by giving him to eat, wealth thinks that it has subjected the other's inmost essence to itself. It disregards the fact that the other is bound to rebel and that his rebellion will be as total as the grab which wealth makes for his essence. In his "pure dismemberment" the poor rejects the opinion of his benefactor, this benefactor himself and even everything that exists. Even as self-consciousness spoke a language to the power of the state, so the poor speak to wealth. This also is a language of flattery, but it is base, it is "the

---

[15] Hegel, *op. cit.*, pp. 148-158.

language of dismemberment." It is only in this language that the spirit of human culture finds full expression. To express the total dismemberment, it says that all opposites mean exactly the same: good *is* evil, generous *is* base.

True, "the tranquil consciousness" will protest when good and evil are identified, but this protest cannot be accepted. It says that although good and evil are indeed commingled, this mixture precisely expresses the wisdom of nature. This protest must be rejected because it make evil a condition of the good. And when the protest points to examples of excellence, it shows that reality is generally the opposite of such solitary exceptions: "The fact that the good is presented as a special 'anecdote' is the most bitter thing one can say of the good." And if the tranquil consciousness demands that the entire evil world be rejected and that man withdraw from this world, then it forgets that Diogenes in his barrel was dependent on his barrel and would not have been Diogenes without it. True, the evil world must be transcended, but not by the individual. What the situation really is can be described as follows.

Now that all opposites merge, the domain of the real world also collapses. Now that everything fixed and permanent is lost, absolute dread arises, even as the slave in his mortal fear experienced "not some kind of anxiety but absolute dread." But absolute dread refers to the world in its entirety. Does the world face its definitive ruin? No, the world faces the revolution which will put an end to estrangement and establish absolute freedom. Estrangement was necessary. This reconciliation is necessary because, as the transcending of all finiteness and opposition, it is its own cause. For, as Spinoza wrote, "By cause of itself I mean that whose very essence includes existence."[16]

The preceding paragraphs show how close Marx remained to Hegel. One no longer needs to ask where Marx obtained his certainty about the coming of the revolution, but at most how he knows that the proletariat is the bearer of history: "The bourgeoisie ... produces ... its own gravediggers. Its fall and the victory of the

---

[16] Hegel, *op. cit.*, pp. 376-405.

proletariat are equally inevitable.[17] Marx freely acknowledges the greatness of Hegel. It lies in this that Hegel conceives the self-development of man as a process, that he understands the essence of work and views man as the result of his own work. But Marx addresses to Hegel the reproach that he conceived man too much as reason, as spirit, too spiritualistically.[18] Marx wishes to do away with the mystifications of Hegel's philosophy of the Spirit, and this can be done only if we make concrete reality our starting point. Of course, Hegel also wished to make this concrete reality intelligible, but for him the concrete is the end-result, built up of elements that must make it intelligible. Marx counters this view by asserting that the concrete must not be handled as an end-result but as the starting point.[19]

Hegel wrongly thinks that only the Spirit is the essence of man. Concrete man lives off inorganic nature, as animals do, but he differs from the animal because he can attain nature in a universal way. Nature is an object of man's consciousness—in physical science and art—and that's why nature is the spiritual nature of man. But nature is also practically a part of human life; it gives man food, heat, clothing and possibilities of shelter. Nature is the "inorganic body" of man; in particular, nature is raw material for man's work, but also the object and tool of his labor. From all this it follows that Hegel has described the process of man's self-realization only in a speculative way. We must realize that the material conditions of life are the true basis of history and that, therefore, they are the norm to be observed by the historian. Man realizes himself as a being of nature; by the same process through which he transforms nature, making it produce, for example, his food, he also transforms himself. The process of self-realization is nothing but concrete human *praxis*.[20]

To understand man, then, requires the understanding of work. Now, according to Marx, Hegel disclosed the essence of work as

---

[17] Marx-Engels, *Manifesto of the Communist Party*, p. 71.
[18] Marx, "Critique of the Hegelian Dialectic and Philosophy as a Whole," *Philosophic and Economic Manuscripts of 1844*, pp. 148 ff.
[19] Marx, *Einleitung zur Kritik der politischen Oekonomie*, vol. 13 in the Dietz Verlag ed. of his *Werke*, p. 632.
[20] Marx, *Pariser Manuscripte* III, in RoRoRo ed. vol. 2, p. 86; *The German Ideology*, New York, 1947, pp. 7, 14 ff.

"the species-consciousness and species-life that comes-to-be." Marx could have referred to a famous passage of Hegel's PHENOMENOLOGY OF MIND, where Hegel formulates the hypothesis that the man who works relates his work only to himself. One who does this wants to prevent others from participating in it. He makes something, but is not so much interested in what he is making as in the fact that it is his work. Is his motive perhaps that he wishes to let the others do their own work? No, as soon as the others accomplish something, he is there to help and thus appropriate it to himself, or to praise it and thus to proclaim his own magnanimity. The hypothesis, then, cannot be maintained. Thus work must be defined as the work of this *and* of all other individuals, as "the work of all and of each."[21] Marx took over this idea. The working man is not an isolated monad but a "species-being." Work is the self-realization of all of us; it realizes all "species-powers."

That's what work *is*; yet that's *not* what work in our capitalistic society is. This discrepancy is possible only if modern work is estranged from its essence. And because the developmental stage of work must correspond to the development of the human being who the worker is, it follows that modern man also is estranged from his essence.

Accordingly, the characteristic element of estranged work is that its product no longer functions for the self-realization of all men. First of all, capital takes the product of work away from the worker; his own product now faces him as an alien, hostile and oppressive power. He therefore also becomes estranged from his work and feels "at home" only when he is not working. And because work is his productive dealing with nature, he also becomes estranged from nature, which is his "species-essence." Finally, because his product belongs to someone else, the worker is estranged from his fellowman.

Unity and reconciliation have been sacrificed to non-identity and opposition in man himself, the opposition between what man is by his essence and what he *de facto* is. This also means that there is opposition between people: they are divided into classes and locked in combat. As a result the state also is adversely affected; it sees no possibility of uniting the opposing classes and opts for the

---

21 *Phänomenologie des Geistes*, p. 377.

ruling class. Philosophy also is estranged, for it does not realize that it is a reflex of an estranged situation. And, of course, religion is an estrangement—"as far as Germany is concerned, the critique of religion is essentially finished"—because it preaches resignation.

Accordingly, salvation is not to be expected from either the State, philosophy or religion. The condition of alienated labor can only be undone by the power of the proletariat, the class that possesses nothing and ought to possess everything. The revolution is the definitive transcendence of the alienation. After the revolution, then, man will be what he essentially is: an integral man, divided neither against himself nor from his fellowmen, Only then democracy will act as the reconciliation of civil society with the State; through this reconciliation civil society will cease being *bourgeois* because it has overcome the egoism of private interests; the State will no longer be a *political* State.

3. *The Essence of Estrangement*

Hegel and Marx range over a realm as wide as the history of the world. It would be impossible here to delve deeper into the problems they raise, but we will return to their rejection of faith and religion in the next chapter. Here we will limit ourselves to the question of the essence of estrangement. From the preceding paragraphs we know that estrangement is something that happens within the world; it is connected with the process of self-realization and is a component element of human historicity. And we recall, without as yet understanding it, that Hegel distinguished two kinds of estrangement. Our analysis must now be pursued by a reflection upon historicity.

The use of the concept "necessary estrangement" enables Hegel and Marx to defend the paradox that man does not cease to realize himself in history and that, nevertheless, history presents the picture of an ever-increasing disorder. For the nesessary estrangement is the negative side of self-realization. By the same token, however, it is not the final end. The equally necessary reconciliation is the power of attraction that puts everything into motion, and this power has been at work from the very beginning. This power has called forth all the forms in which history is clothed; in other words, it is the power which necessitates the estrangement and equally necessitates the revolution. But this means that self-realization must be divided into two phases, the phase before the revolution and the phase after it.

Marx explicitly distinguishes two forms of history. Everything preceding the revolution is merely the genetic history of man; by way of his alienation man is busy becoming the man he truly is. Marx calls this phase "preparatory history." History itself will only begin when the revolution has produced the integral man;[22] then all non-identity will be transcended. That is why the essence of man, once it has been realized, can never be lost again. Hegel doesn't know two kinds of history but only one, the history "of the spirit externalized in time." Nevertheless, even in Hegel we find the problem which interests us here. For the revolution which ends the estrangement marks for him the end of history. It happens at the moment when the spirit in its self-perfection "abolishes time.[23]

The standpoints of Hegel and Marx differ but they manifest the same problematics. In both cases there is a split in man's self-realization. So far as Marx is concerned, we will disregard the question when the final condition will begin. Obviously, it has not yet become a reality. Prominent Marxist philosophers, such as Schaff, deny the possibility of a human situation in which alienation would no longer play a role.[24] Their reason is that man always remains within the typical human historicity. Must we say, then, with Hegel that everything is history? Yes, provided we deny that history itself is on the road to its own extermination. The absolute reconciliation, in which all non-identity is transcended, doesn't lie within human history, not even as the end of history. Absolute identity doesn't belong to man, for he is finite. Man is a transcending movement in which the facticity of the ego and of the world is transcended toward a new possibility; this possibility will be a purer approximation—but only an approximation—of what man and the world authentically are. That's why opposition, as the opposition of facticity and authenticity, is *essential* to man. As a transcending movement, man is characterized by historicity. The

---

[22] "Private Property and Communism," *Economic and Philosophic Manuscripts of 1844*, p. 102.

[23] Hegel, *op. cit.*, pp. 169, 612.

[24] A. Schaff, *Marxismus und das menschliche Individuum*, Vienna, 1965.

opposition in question, then, is essential to his historicity. And as such it is not yet an alienation.

But we know now where the possibility of alienation arises and what its essence is. If man is a transcending movement, estrangement is the immobilization of this movement. In every stage of man's self-realization, says Beerling, he is tempted to listen to the Mephistophelian invitation: "Please stay, you are so beautiful." "We could call 'estrangement' the condition that arises when the process of externalization and mediation stagnates and man resigns himself to what has already been achieved, acquired or made available, thus expiring as *homo viator*, as one who is on the way. Considered in this fashion, alienation must be equated with a condition of non-dialectic stagnation."[25]

Starting with Hegel, we made a distinction between two kinds of alienation, one that functions positively in man's self-realization and one that functions there negatively. Which of these two did we refer to in the preceding pages? The immobilization that goes counter to man as a progressive movement evidently is the negative alienation. It is no coincidence that this negative kind revealed itself first in our analysis, for the negative estrangement is the alienation which really contradicts man in his essence.

4. The Primary Forms of Estrangement

To discover the forms in which the alienation primarily occurs we must realize that the ego should develop in freedom toward its own form, but that the starting point of this process is determined by the typical situation of helplessness. For every human being is born in a helpless condition. The new-born child is a new human being not merely because he is new-born but also because never was one born like him and never again will there be one like him. He is characterized by his unique ownness.

But what sense does it make to speak of this child's ownness? He does not yet know anything, cannot yet do anything; how, then, could he go his own way? Without the care of his parents and all the others who look after him, he would be lost. His parents act for him and speak for him, and they show him how to act and speak.

---

25 R. F. Beerling, *Wijsgerig-sociologische verkenningen*, vol. I, p. 107.

The child is ready to do as they do, he shows a strong urge to imitate. Let us add that before long another urge will manifest itself, the urge to say "no" and to be contrary. He has then reached the "age of defiance" and will go through several stages of saying "no."

What does it mean that the child must be guided and aided by his parents? He cannot yet help himself. We may describe this by saying that the child, although he *is* a standpoint of his own, does not yet know his ownness; he does not yet know who he is. That's why he is dependent. This gives rise to a problem: the child must be aided by his parents, but even the parents don't know who he is. They know, of course, that he is their child, but this merely indicates who he is for his parents, not who the child *himself* is as this new man. The parents cannot know who their child is because their child is another human being and therefore different than themselves. The conclusion following from this is that the parents lead the child in a direction which is *never exactly* that of the child himself.

This situation should not be dramatized, for it belongs to the natural course of human development. But at the same time it shows that we meet here an alienation which we have not yet encountered in our analysis, viz., the alienation that functions positively in man's self-realization. In line with Hegel we could describe this positive alienation as the necessity for man to leave his natural immediacy, to widen his horizon, or as Hegel says, to gain a real "extension." This means—no longer in line with Hegel—that if man is ever to be able to extend his interests beyond the realm enclosed by his own skin, then others must forcibly lead him to the domain of otherness.

Positive alienation, let us repeat it, is not alienation in the true sense of the term. Yet it makes sense to speak here of alienation in order to express that man doesn't have a pure beginning. We have come across this conclusion at an earlier point, namely after we had rejected the Platonic view of man and the Platonic conception of creation. But at that stage this conclusion was still premature, for one could have brought to bear against it the scholastic thesis that man has no innate ideas but begins as a *tabula rasa*, a blank writing tablet. The suggestion of a virgin beginning, however, that lies in the comparison with the blank sheet of paper is meaningful only in a philosophy which ascribes the primacy to the intellect. As we have seen, this primacy must be assigned to the movement of transcendence. Once a philosophy recognizes this point, it doesn't come in contradiction with the conclusion that man doesn't have a pure beginning.

What exactly is meant by this assertion that man doesn't have a pure beginning? The concept "positive alienation" expresses that the above-described situation makes alienation in the strict sense possible, even though this situation as such is not an invitation to estrangement but to self-realization. It is as if there has to be an intermediary between the positivity of the human essence and the negativity of alienation in the strict sense, and this intermediary is the positive alienation. Let us, then, see how estrangement in the strict sense is now made possible.

When the ego is forcibly moved to the realm of otherness by the positive alienation, this very fact contains the possibility that the ego will definitively settle there. But in this case it will never come to itself, at least not to its authentic self. The ego then lets itself be determined by the others and therefore doesn't come to be as the free, self-determining being which it is. Heidegger would add that this is an advantage rather than an obstacle to the ego's participation in public life. For the ego, which in this way has cut itself off from its own intensity, covers a large realm of otherness by means of the "extension" already achieved by the others. One who doesn't come to be himself doesn't distinguish himself from the others, but is one of them. This is the situation in which everyone is the other and no one is himself, the situation of inauthenticity in its first form. This first form of estrangement in the strict sense, then, may be described as the immobilization of my self-movement which arises when I let myself be determined by someone else, when I let the others take away my self-determination.

It should be pointed out that this estrangement also occurs when I submit to general laws and regulations without taking any personal position. General moral and religious convictions should be included in this statement. There is no need to be alarmed by this. One who lets himself be determined by general moral or religious

convictions is not a moral or religious man, for the simple reason
that morality and religiousness imply self-determination. To a morality of a religion accepted without personally taking a position we
can fully apply Marx's claim that both are alienations.

Moreover, one should clearly understand what is meant when
one uses the concept "general law." General laws don't originate in
a vacuum and don't speak to me from a vacuum. They are laws
that express the unity of the norm, but they express this unity as
interpreted by the one who speaks. The consequences of the idea
of interpretation make themselves felt here.[26] Now, the interpretation which someone else gives to a norm that is also my norm can
never be *exactly* my interpretation of the same norm, for the
simple reason that the other person is someone else and that I am
other than him.

This first form of genuine estrangement we will call "conformism." Conservatism is contained in conformism as one of its vari-
ations. For, as we saw, man is progressive as transcending movement and conservative insofar as he takes his universal concepts
and judgments out of the transcending movement which he is,
sets them up in isolation and fixes them. But to fix is to immobilize.
We now understand how the conservative man is possible. Man
is progressive, he is *not* conservative. This means that the conservative man is possible only as an estrangement of man's essence.
More specifically, this is the first form of estrangement in the strict
sense precisely because the conservative man ascribes a free-
floating validity to universal concepts and judgments; he doesn't
realize that these concepts and judgments were of necessity formulated in terms of a certain interpretation and that they demand,
with the same necessity, a personal interpretation.

If the ego may not let the others take away its self-
determination, does it have to oppose itself to the others with a
total and definitive "no"? By such a "no" the ego would, insofar as
possible, undo the fact that it has been forcibly located in the
domain of otherness. Having to arrive at its own interpretation, it
rejects the other; it thereby loses its "extension." Regarding its

---

[26] Concerning the unity of the norm and the genuine pluriformity of its interpretation, see p. 54.

intensity, let us keep in mind that the ego has said "no" to the others, but that these others don't cease to exist because of this "no." In other words, the ego is now in conflict with the others. But the conflict in question is a particular one, a conflict that arose from the ego's "no" and that continues as this same "no" to the other and to everything the other puts forth. How does the ego experience such a conflict?

The ego experiences the opposition contained in the conflict but not the other who is opposed, for the latter is rejected. The ego feels hurt because the other thinks differently than itself, but it is aware only of its own hurt and not of the other. Now, one who doesn't experience the meaning the other has is locked up in his own meaning. And one who experiences only his own hurt becomes lonely through the conflict. No impulse emanating from the realm of otherness still penetrates into him. His intensity ultimately is only the intensity of his hurt and loneliness. For this reason we would like to describe this second form of genuine estrangement as the immobilization of my self-movement which arises when I repel the other and the essence of which lies in the fact that I no longer receive any impulses from the realm of otherness.

In this situation universal validity loses all meaning because there is nothing that can be accepted as holding for both the ego and the other. Accordingly, it isn't merely a matter of denying that the other's interpretation is valid also for me—such a denial is right—but of denying that I and the other ought to be orientated to the same normativity.

The first form of estrangement in the strict sense, which rejects the personal taking of a position, is, we said, the place to which the conservative must be assigned. The second form we may describe as the realm of rebellion. Admittedly, the term "rebellion" can have a positive sense, but that's not what we are concerned with here. For lack of a better word we use the term "rebellion" here to mean the total and undifferentiated "no." Rebellion, then, also is an estrangement from man's progressive essence. It cannot be excluded that some people who are considered progressives, in reality should be classified as rebels.

Finally, we discover the connection between the three categories of conservative, progressive, and rebel, on the one hand, and the three categories disclosed by the analysis of the hermeneutic situation. In hermeneutic terms the conservative is one who indulges in fundamentalistic objectivism; the rebel is one who lapses into the subjectivism of "reading something into the text"; and the progressive is to be identified with the interpreter who both contributes his ownness and accepts that he is subject to norms. Let us now consider the idea that the progressive man is the authentic man.

5. *Authenticity*

If the other's interpretation may not deprive the ego of its self-determination, then the ego ought to say "no" to the other's interpretation. Because the two interpretations ought to be different, this difference will now and then manifest itself and put the two interpretations into opposition. Conflict with the other is inevitable. But this conflict must not run its course in the same way as the conflict of a rebel. The ego must not limit itself to its own hurt but will really listen to the other; it will really let him speak. I let it come about that the other's interpretation stands opposed to mine, I accept the full reality of the conflict. If this is done, then the conflict will reveal itself as fruitful. For every human being still searches for a clarification of his own position, for the truth about himself. The conflict shows where the boundaries are and defines each one's position in reference to those of the others. The other doesn't know who I am, yet he helps me to the truth about myself. And I don't know the other in his own being, yet I bring him to his truth.

How this is possible becomes clearer if we keep in mind that the conflict is of the same nature as the clash constituting the essence of the hermeneutic experience.[27] Even now, when I am clashing with the other's interpretation, I am dealing with the strangeness of a truth which I recognize despite its strangeness: strangeness because of the difference in interpretation, recognition because we speak differently on the basis of the same normative truth. The two aspects, then, of the hermeneutic situation occur also here.

First of all, the truth of the other is not my truth, and that's precisely why I begin to reflect upon my truth; I realize the

---

[27] Cf. pp. 49 ff.

standpoint from which I have arrived at my truth and begin to have an inkling of the different standpoint occupied by the other. This means that the complex of my pre-judices is no longer motionless, so that the danger of immobilization has again been overcome for some time. Some of my pre-judices will be unmasked in my renewed reflection upon my truth, so that I have to *revise* my interpretation. Others I will recognize as specifically mine, but I realize that I may *not absolutize* my interpretation in them. And I also understand that certain pre-judices can be common to both the other and myself, so that they will not be disclosed by our conflict. In such a case I cannot exclude that subsequently they will be contradicted in another encounter with a different fellowman. And this reminds me that I may not consider my interpretation as *definitive.* Finally, if all my efforts to throw light on the conflict by means of the truth under discussion fail, then and only then I try to understand the other's view in psychological terms.

The second aspect of the hermeneutical situation also applies to the conflict. For the other the conflict means that I bring him to a "plus" of truth, just as a text does when it is read. Introduced by me to my interpretation, he is delivered from the incompleteness of his truth. With me he becomes more himself. But this means that the fundamental attitude of the authentic man is good-will toward his fellowmen, love in its fundamental form of "will to promote" the other (Nédoncelle).

If we wish to see what the notion of authentic man means, we should realize how far it is removed from the medieval concept of the genuine man, the *homo verax. Homo verax* speaks the truth and is reliable. What he says agrees with what he thinks; he lives up to his promises; he does not act ambiguously, for he has purified his motives and follows them. In short, he is a just man.

This touching description is based on two presuppositions which, today, we can no longer share. It tacitly assumes that man knows the truth already and that he merely has to speak and act in conformity with the known truth. Truth is no problem; at most, it is a problem for weak man to be faithful to the known truth. Secondly, because the fixed and immutable truth is already known, the fellowman plays no role in man's "veracity." Man achieves this veracity by God's grace and his own efforts, but not by way of his fellowmen.

If, however, truth must be *my* truth and if my life is precisely a search for my truth, truth is no longer to be taken for granted. It is, of course, much simpler to take things as they come, to enjoy the pleasures that present themselves and to abstain from asking *myself* any troublesome questions. Questions will arise even then, but they are easy to live with if I am satisfied with the answers others have given to them. I stop looking for my own standpoint and rely on ready-made answers. This is not only much simpler but also much safer and takes away the risk that I will make a mistake and go the wrong way. Every risk implies a certain anxiety, which is something disagreeable. To avoid anxiety, I must stick to the established paths.

The authentic man, however, is one who dares to face the fact that there is no established path for him. It is true, of course, that innumerable trails have been blazed through life, but this was done by other people. His own path of life has not yet been blazed; he himself must cut it out from the forest of possibilities presenting themselves.

But the authentic man is not a solitary individual who rejects his fellowman. Because of his attitude, he cannot avoid conflict with his fellowman, but he accepts this risk because he knows that this conflict is fruitful. He knows that he cannot simply take over what his fellowman tells him, but he also knows that nothing of what this fellowman says will ever be wholly meaningless. The authentic man allows himself to be contradicted, stimulated to renewed reflection on things which he considered permanent acquisitions. He has opted for the difficult life. In this way he is faithful to the truth that his truth is not a possession but a process of development. At every moment of this process truth is attained, for without truth life is impossible, but every acquired truth always remains mobile.

CHAPTER SEVEN

"At Home" Or In "A Strange Country"?

Religion can have an alienating influence—namely, when one takes over the accepted religious conviction, without taking any personal position. But Marx goes much farther than this; for him religion, as such, is an alienation. In Marx's view man *is* areligious, so that religiousness is only possible as an alienation of the human being. This topic will be considered in this chapter, but we will limit ourselves here to the fundamental sense of religiousness. Its full sense will occupy us in the final chapter, where we will try to show that a philosophy can speak in a meaningful way about the Creator-God.

One who approaches this question after reading Marx cannot disregard the problem of secularization. For secularization can be described as the process in which God is cast out from the world, so that the world at last can become a world and man can finally feel at home in the world (Luijpen). Secularization, at any rate, is a protest against the Platonic-Augustinian idea that man's earthly life is an alienation.

Hegel's description of faith strongly resembles Augustine's sketch of earthly life. But while Augustine concludes that earthly life is merely a means that shouldn't be enjoyed, Hegel concludes that the believer becomes estranged from his essence. The fundamental ideas of Hegel's philosophy, we may add, could be described as a secularization of theological concepts. In this way absolute reconciliation becomes a secularized eschatology, and the Spirit who must become self-alienated is a secularization of the incarnation, self-emptying and crucifixion of Christ. Hegel's conviction that the opposition between the finite and the infinite must be overcome has exercised a strong influence upon the contemporary aversion to a transcendent God.

With respect to Marx himself, his "messianism" is a point to which attention is often drawn. Following Feuerbach, Marx declares that the existence of religion is a sign that the world has not yet come to itself, so that asking about religion is asking about the world: "We convert theological questions into secular questions."[1] History as it has run its course till the present is man's genetic history, says Marx, and this means that man is born from himself, so that the question of creation has become impossible.[2] Man creates himself. That's why Prometheus, who stole the fire from the gods and thus made it possible for man to establish himself in the world as his home and develop his potential, "ranks first among the saints and martyrs in the calendar of philosophy."[3]

Let us keep in mind that scholastic thought was strongly marked with the idea of *theoria* or contemplation, and let us assume—without presenting any proof for it here—that Christian *praxis* has always been strongly affected by a defeatist Platonism. Now, if this kind of thinking and this kind of *praxis* are confronted with the mentality of the contemporary man who seizes control of his own situation, one can understand why the Christian God is no longer heard in the modern world. Nietzsche describes this situation in the contrast between Zarathustra and the old saint. Coming down from the mountain where for ten years he has enjoyed his spirit and his solitude, Zarathustra returns to the people because he has gathered so much wisdom that he is like a bee that has gathered too much honey and needs outstretched hands to take it. The first person whom he meets is an old man, a saint who has fled away from people to the solitude of the forest. "And what doeth the saint in the forest?" asked Zarathustra. The saint answered: "I make hymns and sing them. . . ; thus I praise God." As soon as Zarathustra was

---

[1] "On the Jewish Question," *Writings of the Young Marx*, p. 223.

[2] "Private Property and Communism," *Philosophic and Economic Manuscripts of 1844*, p. 113.

[3] Preface to his doctoral dissertation, Marx-Engels *Gesamtausgabe*, vol. 1. part 1, Berlin, 1927, p. 10.

alone, however, he said to himself: "Could it be possible? This old saint in the forest hath not yet heard of it, that God is dead."[4]

1. *"People Are so Unashamedly at Home"*

The contemporary Christian is aware of the process of secularization, not because of Nietzsche, but because of a thinker who was able to achieve greater prestige among Christians than Nietzsche could—namely, Dietrich Bonhoeffer.

The central theme of Bonhoeffer is that man has come of age and is autonomous. Man has discovered the laws governing the course of the world. Ethics no longer speaks of divine commandments but of rules of life. Since Macchiavelli politics is independent of morality and follows its own laws. Hugo Grotius formulated a code of international law that is valid "even if God doesn't exist." And in Descartes' philosophy the world has become a machine that works as it should without any divine intervention. Spinoza, Kant, Fichte and Hegel think in the direction of man's autonomy. Now that man knows the laws of the world, he can take care of himself in all important matters; he doesn't need to appeal to God as a "working hypothesis."

God has been abolished and overcome as a moral, political or scientific working hypothesis. Intellectual honesty demands that man drop such an hypothesis or at least eliminate it as much as possible. It has become obvious that things work also without God and no less well than they used to. This applies not only to the above-mentioned realms but to the entire range of man's endeavors: God "in losing ground," He is more and more pulled out of the world. And while God is losing ground, the world gains a certainty which nothing can shake. True, sometimes the world develops in the wrong direction, not every effort is crowned with success; but such failures, including the present world war, are soberly and manly accepted, they don't affect the certainty that the world is developing of necessity and in the right direction.

Both Catholics and Protestants, says Bonhoeffer, view this development as the great apostasy from God. They anxiously ask,

---

[4] Nietzsche, *Thus Spake Zarathustra*, Prologue, in *The Philosophy of Nietzsche*, Modern Library Edition, pp. 5-6.

"Where does any room remain for God?" In former times people brought God to bear upon any realm where man's knowledge fell short. But now that man expands his boundaries ever more by his own power, there is very little room left for God's exclusive domain. Yet those people still try to "sell" to man, now that has come of age, the idea that he cannot live without God as his guardian. They have capitulated in all secular questions, but, so they say, there remain the ultimate questions—of death and guilt— and with respect to these only God can give an answer. Or else they try to prove to the happy and contented man that he is really unhappy and suffering from an unrecognized need. They endeavor to drive man to despair in order to triumph over him, they try "to sabotage him religiously." Or, finally they trust that man's "religious *a priori*" will always continue to exist.

Bonhoeffer isn't satisfied with this kind of answer. It could easily happen that sooner or later it will become evident that this "religious *a priori*" does not at all exist. Or perhaps it will become evident that those so-called ultimate questions don't exist or that they can be answered without God. God is not a "stop-gap." He doesn't fill the gaps existing in our knowledge and power. The attacks of Christian apologists on man's autonomy, says Bonhoeffer, are senseless, tasteless and unchristian.

They are senseless because one cannot force an adult to become again a puber. One cannot make him again dependent on things on which he is no longer dependent, causing him to experience problems where he no longer has any problems. It is tasteless because one misuses the weakness of a person for purposes foreign to him. One declares that what is most intimate to man—from his prayer to his sexuality—is the hunting domain of modern pastoral care, thereby doing exactly the same as the yellow press. Finally, it is unchristian because one confuses Christ with a particular phase of man's religiousness which today's adult man has outgrown.

That's why this kind of apologetics must be stopped. It is time to recognize, says Bonhoeffer in his most important conclusion, that modern man is religionless. But this religionless adult is perhaps closer to God than man has ever been before he came of age.

The reason why we are referring here to Bonhoeffer lies in his topic that man has come of age. The adult man is religionless, but we should realize here that Bonhoeffer uses the term "religion" is a very special and restricted sense. The religious man, as Bonhoeffer understands him—an understanding that owes much to Karl Barth—proceeds on the basis of a separation between the internal and the external life of man. His external life is secular, but the internal, the intimate life of man is religious. Bonhoeffer protests that this separation is unbiblical and implies that the religious man can never be a whole man, an integral man, but will always be only a partial man. But in that case Christ can never become the Lord of the world.

For Bonhoeffer the religious man is an individualist, intent on the salvation of his own soul, who has already given up on the world. That's why, in Bonhoeffer's eyes, religion is the opposite of an integral acceptance of God and the world. The religious man is only half a man, but the Christian must be a whole man. Most symptomatic of all is perhaps Bonhoeffer's complaint that he finds it so difficult to speak about God with religious people while on the other hand he can do this spontaneously with non-religious men. He finds it so difficult, I think, because the religious man knows already who God is, he has God at his disposal, "possesses" Him.[5]

Let us return to our topic of man as having come of age. If man has come of age and discovered the laws governing the world, so that he now can take care of himself, doesn't it follow with an inexorable necessity that man is at home in the world? Yet we find a curious expression in Bonhoeffer. His book WIDERSTAND UND ER-GEBUNG is mainly composed of letters written to his friend Eberhard Bethge. Bethge's own letters to Bonhoeffer are not contained in it. But in one of his letters Bonhoeffer returns to an expression used by Bethge and says: "I wholeheartedly approve your expression: 'People are so quickly and unashamedly at home.' I am going to steal this expression from you; I am going to borrow and use it."[6] Bonhoeffer, then, agrees that people are quickly and unashamedly

---

[5] D. Bonhoeffer, *Widerstand und Ergebung*, Munich, 1962, see especially pp. 215-221.

[6] *Op. cit.*, p. 143.

at home. But how can one say that man is unashamedly at home? Hasn't he come of age? If he has, then he is at home in the world.

2. Hegel's Interpretation of Modern History

Accordingly, it is wrong to claim, in line with Platonism, that man estranges himself from God if he considers the world as his home. Hegel's critique of faith actually is a critique of this Platonic view of Christianity. The same can be asserted about Marx's critique of religion. And Nietzsche laughs at the old saint who loves God but not man because man "is a thing too imperfect for me." Finally, Bonhoeffer criticizes the religious man because he has already given up the world as lost.

Man, then, is the being who more and more establishes himself in the world as his home. But the question is how this development of man must be described. One point is certain in this matter. Let's see this first.

Man who has developed physical science and technology, as a matter of principle no longer recognizes any areas as "off limits" in the world. He penetrates everywhere. Through his modern means of communication he can be present anywhere in the world in a very short time. The map of the world no longer has any blank spots. At least in principle man has pressed the whole of nature into his service. Hereafter we will express this idea by saying that man has taken possession of the world in its total *extension*.

Now it is precisely this development that seems to worry many Christians. For, the reader will recall, Bonhoeffer describes a similar process when he says that God is more and more pushed into the background both in science and in life; He is "losing ground." In the world that has come of age God no longer has any realm of His own, any realm from which man is excluded. No part of the world is any longer foreign to man. Accordingly, if the question, "Where is there still room for God?" is understood literally, the answer is, "Nowhere."

The question, however, which concerns us can only now be formulated properly: Does man's coming home mean the definitive elimination of *every* kind of strangeness? One would perhaps be inclined to answer in the affirmative and say that every form of

strangeness is increasingly overcome. At the end it will be totally
eliminated. Man is on the way toward a situation in which no
strangeness at all will continue to exist. But we will have to reflect
upon this answer to see whether or not it is correct.

Is it really true that modern history can be integrally characterized as the movement in which man increasingly "comes home" by
eliminating *all* strangeness, in other words, not merely strangeness
in the sense of extension? How did we arrive at that view? Did we
observe its truth for ourselves? But all we did observe was that
man establishes himself over the entire *extension* of the world. And
if we didn't observe it ourselves, we arrived at that view by taking
it over from someone else. But in that case were we justified in
doing this?

To begin with the first point, it was Hegel who proposed the
interpretation that modern history is the development in which
man totally eliminates every form of strangeness from the world. In
Hegel's philosophy the world arose as a self-estrangement of the
Spirit; and that's why the Spirit returns to itself by transcending
every form of strangeness.

The way Hegel looks at Descartes eloquently illustrates his standpoint. Let us keep in mind that Descartes is of particular importance for the problems occupying us here. A prominent mathematician, he was one of the founders of the modern physical science
which enabled us to make the world subservient to our needs. But
Descartes is particularly important as the philosopher of the *cogito*.
He stands at the beginning of the modern attitude of mind which
bases the world on the self-sure ego. That's why Descartes opens
the period of man's coming of age. Now, Hegel's appreciation of
Descartes is extremely positive. In his eyes, Descartes is an essential moment in the "home-coming" of the Spirit. In Descartes, says
Hegel, we find for the first time an autonomous philosophy, "standing on its own ground" and no longer a philosophizing theology.
"Here we are at home; like a captain ending a long voyage on a
stormy sea, we can exclaim here 'land.' " For with Descartes a
philosophy arose which rejects the dead exteriority of authority and
bases itself upon interiority; man began to think in freedom. Anything which must be held as a truth in the world is something that

man must have understood through his reflection. Hence we are "at
home" in this philosophy, for "everyone is originally a thinking
being."[7]

All we have gained from this is at least a few interesting viewpoints. We know now that Hegel's view of modern history is an
interpretation. The fact that it is an interpretation means that other
interpretations are possible, for the notion of "the only possible
interpretation" is a contradiction in terms. This leads us to consider
another interpretation of modern history, viz., that of Heidegger.
Secondly, we are now confronted with a strange fact. If we viewed
modern history as a development in which man wholly eliminates
all strangeness from the world, we would be going along with
Hegel's philosophy. As a matter of fact, however, the hermeneutics
sketched in Chapters Five and Six is precisely an implicit critique
of Hegel's idea that strangeness can ever be totally eliminated.
These two points deserve our attention here.

3. Heidegger's Interpretation of Modern History

In one of his essays published in HOLZWEGE Heidegger tries to
understand the modern era. He recognizes science as one of the
essential phenomena of this era. Science, he says, is first of all
research. This means that the mind opens a certain domain to
itself. Science begins with a project which prescribes how the
knowing mind must approach its domain and therefore also determines how things will reveal themselves within science. This
prescription secures the rigorous character of the research. At the
same time, however, it determines the outline of what still may be
called "nature," viz., the self-contained complex-of-motions of spa-
tio-temporally interconnected masses. This outline of nature a priori makes a number of decisions; for instance, that motion is merely
a change in position and that all motions are equivalent. Accordingly, physical science is not exact because it calculates so
carefully; on the contrary, it must calculate very carefully because
its bond with the domain of its research is characterized by ex-

---

[7] Hegel, *Vorlesungen über die Geschichte der Philosophie: Descartes*, in
Glockner ed. of Hegel's works, vol. 15, p. 328.

actness. *Geisteswissenschaft* is also characterized by the rigorousness of its bond with its domain, but this rigorousness precisely doesn't assume the form of exactness.

Secondly, science is a procedure, a way of acting. If relevant facts are to occur within the domain opened by science, then one must first formulate a law through which the facts can be explained and this law itself must be affirmed or denied by the facts. That's why every experiment presupposes a law as the condition under which the fact can be calculated beforehand. This law isn't, of course, a product of arbitrariness, but is formulated strictly in accordance with the fundamental plan of nature which science has already laid down. The experiment of physical science has its counterpart in the critique of the sources in *Geisteswissenschaft;* one tries to find, safeguard, evaluate, preserve and explain the sources. To explain means here to compare everything with everything else. Only that which can be compared can be object of science here. In the constant comparison of everything with everything else one "figures out" what can be understood. But anything unique, rare or great remains inexplicable, save as an exception.

Thirdly, modern science is an "enterprise," it only begins to look like a science if it can create a special institute with its own research apparatus. This is symptomatic of the fact that science is not interested without any limitation in all the facts accumulating around us. It more and more addresses itself to those specific possibilities to which it gave itself access when it laid down its fundamental plan. The implication of this is that the scientific procedure has priority over the object of the science, that is, the procedure has priority over nature in physical science and over history in *Geisteswissenschaft.* This phenomenon is paralleled by the fact that the scholar disappears and is replaced by the man of research who no longer needs a library at home: he works at his institute, travels to congresses, delivers lectures or writes a book at the request of a publisher.

Heidegger wonders about the metaphysical conceptions underlying modern science, conceptions about being and truth. "Knowing which has become research demands an account (*Rechenschaft*) of being as to how and to what extent it can be at our disposal." Research disposes of being when it pre-calculates its future course or checks its past subsequently. "Calculating before" and "calculating subsequently" are characteristic of physical science and of *Geisteswissenschaft* respectively. Nature and history thus become the object of explanatory representation: "the former counts on nature, the latter counts with history." Only that which in this way *is* object qualifies as *being*. And it becomes object in a representation which puts every being before us in such a way that the calculating man can be certain of this being. *Truth* is the certainty of the representation.

This is the background of modern science and therefore also of modern history. Of course, one can also say that man has liberated himself from his medieval restriction. (Heidegger means this as a reference to Hegel, but abstains from naming him.) Such an interpretation, however, remains superficial and disregards what is essential in the phenomenon. This essential element is the tacit decision made by man when he assumed the attitude of modern science. Man thereby decided that he was the one on whom all beings are founded and to whom all have to render an account. Thus he became "the center to which everything refers." Man now is the calculator, something now *is* only insofar as it *calculable* and something is *true* only insofar as man has been able to put it before himself. Man is the measure of everything, he is the being "which measures all being and lays down the norm for it."

Heidegger argues against this decision. Man must pursue science and he is therefore entitled to calculating what-is. But he is wrong when he thinks that *Being* and *being-calculable* may be equated and therefore he makes a mistake in his self-definition. That's why he must renew his reflections, to discover again that Being really is "the incalculable." To preserve "the incalculable" in its truth is something which can only be done by one who in authentic reflection knows how to ask creative questions and how to evoke creative forms. This reflection places man in an "in between" in which, on the one hand, he "belongs to Being" and, on the other, "remains a stranger among the beings."[8]

Significantly, Heidegger's interpretation of Descartes is much less

---

[8] Heidegger, "Die Zeit des Weltbildes," *Holzwege*, Frankfurt a.M., 1957, pp. 69-105.

positive than that given by Hegel. Descartes "must be overcome."
The entire modern metaphysics, including that of Nietzsche, is
marked by the explanation of being and truth given by Descartes.
Thus overcoming Descartes means overcoming the entire modern
metaphysics.[9]

All this means that another interpretation of modern history is
possible. Man's home-coming is understood here as the calculating
seizure of power over nature and history. Heidegger's interpretation
doesn't deny science or that man "comes home" in this way.
For man *de facto* takes possession of the world in its entire *extension*. But Heidegger denies that Being is calculable in its entire
intensity and can be possessed by man in this way. If we recognize
that Being cannot be reduced to its calculable aspects, if we recognize the depth of Being and reflect upon it, we realize that man
cannot, in the final analysis, be the measure of everything, that the
inmost depth of beings escape him and remains strange for him,
and that man himself, in spite of his "home-coming," "remains a
stranger among the beings."

4. Hermeneutic Experience Implies Strangeness

Heidegger's interpretation of modern history doesn't merely reach
a different conclusion than Hegel, but in Heidegger's typical way it
also discloses a truth of history which had escaped Hegel. The
picture of history painted by Hegel undoubtedly is grand; it allots
a place to all other philosophies as stages in the self-movement of
the Spirit which finds its completion in Hegel's own philosophy.
In other words, Hegel merges everything previously thought-out
into a new synthesis. If Heidegger had proceeded in the same way,
he would have taken over Hegel's interpretation of history and completed it further by adding the reflections made since then. But
that's not what Heidegger does. He puts forward other truths, his
attention doesn't go to what has already been thought-out but
precisely to what has not yet been reflected upon. "The 'unthought'
is the task of thinking and it continues forever to give rise to

---

9 Heidegger, *op. cit.*, p. 92.

thought. The 'unthought' will never totally merge into the 'thought.' "¹⁰

But this conviction can readily be recognized as the foundation of our hermeneutics, which let's add, owes much to Heidegger. The interpreter, we said, must overcome the strangeness of the truth which, nonetheless, he recognized, by introducing it into his own project. In this way the incomplete truth of the text is brought to greater completion. This completion is possible because the interpreter, having become conscious of his own standpoint, begins to see the standpoint from which the text speaks. That's to say, he recognizes its pre-judices. But a pre-judice is precisely that which has not yet been thought out. The completion brought about by the interpretation is the thinking out of what has not yet been thought out.

Even after this interpretation, however, the text continues to demand further completion. No interpretation is definitive; any allegedly definitive interpretation is simply an alienation of man's interpretative essence. Every new reader will be able to recognize the truth of the text, but at the same time this truth will also appear strange to him. The strangeness of the text cannot be transcended; the hermeneutic situation cannot be overcome. The reason is that it is a situation of the reader himself, so that he can never fully put himself *at a distance* from it.

That's why we say that the reader has an experience in reading the text, a hermeneutic experience. But, as Gadamer rightly says, experience refers primarily to that which I do *not* expect because it goes beyond my expectations, doesn't come up to them or simply is different from what I expect. That's the kind of experience we acquire. When we acquire an experience, it becomes evident that hitherto we didn't see things and people in the right way and that only now we realize how matters stand: "they are different from what we thought." Experience usually implies disappointment. I "learn," of course, from my experiences, but this doesn't primarily mean that I acquire new insights on a conceptual level, even though it is true that insights result from my experience. An experienced man isn't one who knows everything already, but one who is totally undogmatic because he has reached the stage where he

---

¹⁰ S. Ijsseling, *Heidegger*, Antwerp, 1964, p. 31.

remains open to the most unexpected. The primary fruit of experience is that from now on I will be more open to experience itself.
Experience is experience of man's finiteness, so that man is again
and again confronted with the unexpected. This assertion should
also be seen in contrast to Hegel. Experience teaches man that he
"is not the lord of history."[11]

From all this we realize that Hegel's interpretation of modern
history is one-sided and disregards the fact that man stands in
history as a finite being. Because man is finite, the strangeness
beings possess in their inmost nature is a strangeness which remains
with them forever.

5. The Two Aspects of the Cogito

To terminate these considerations, let us try to understand how
Hegel could be so one-sided. We can start again with his interpretation of Descartes. Hegel obviously was fascinated by the philosophy
of the *cogito*, for it was the first philosophy to contain a development toward genuine self-consciousness. The *cogito*, however, contains two aspects, but Hegel paid attention to only one of them.

"I think, therefore, I am," says Descartes. It cannot be denied
that I think, for to deny is to think. Thus it is equally impossible to
deny that I am. This certainty cannot be put in doubt. And that's
why, in Descartes' eyes, the self-certain ego can function as a
foundation for certainty about the world. But the *cogito* has also
another aspect. The certainty that I am does not at all imply who I
am, I as this unrepeatable individual. I must still search for my
own self, I must still interpret myself. This interpretation will never
be definitive, I'll never know definitively who I am. To this extent I
remain a stranger for myself.

But is this assertion tenable? For no one is as close to me as I
myself. True, but I cannot fail to observe that to a large extent I
remain non-transparent to myself. I know, of course, my name, and
the function I exercise; I can also enumerate all the exact data
contained in my description. I can ascribe all kinds of general
qualities to myself. But when I live authentically, I know that I am

---

[11] Gadamer, *Wahrheit und Methode,* pp. 339-340.

not circumscribed by a list of general qualities. It is then that I face the question: Who am I?

But how is it possible that I don't know who I am? Man is free; that's why, in Sartre's language, man disposes in freedom of his own essence. A chair "has" an essence, which is fixed once and for all. A chair "is" what it is, no more and no less. But man is a being who makes himself in freedom be the one he is. According to this line of thought, I must know who I am; I am only what I myself make of myself.

As we will see in the following chapter, this line of thought is incomplete. But here we are interested only in this question: if man in total freedom makes himself be the one he is, how is it possible that he doesn't know who he is?

This situation is conceivable only if man is a transcending movement in the sense we have described, if the ego is constantly busy with re-interpreting itself. For in that case every interpretation is an interpretation of something that forever needs to be interpreted again, viz., my authentic ego. I can never exhaustively interpret my authentic ego, and to this extent I remain a stranger for myself.

Hegel paid attention to the first aspect of the *cogito*. That's why he concentrated on the familiarity with which I am at home with myself. In the perspective of his total "home-coming" man is the being on whom everything is founded and who develops into the measure of all things. Heidegger is more sensitive to the second aspect of the *cogito*. On the basis of our hermeneutics we can now see the deficiencies of Hegel and recognize the inescapable strangeness which remains hidden in the depth of all beings. That's why we reject the idea that man, who in science rightly makes all beings refer to himself, can be *defined* as "the center of reference." In the following chapter we will reflect more explicitly on the fact that not only a reader but man as man is subject to norms. First, however, we must give an answer to the questions raised in the introduction to this chapter.

6. Man's Fundamental Religiousness

We are searching for man's religiousness but, as was mentioned before, in this chapter we will not yet discuss the full meaning of religiousness but only its fundamental dimension. This dimension has now been reached. Man *is* religious because man himself is not the norm of everything, but stands open to all beings in their intensity, their strangeness, which with respect to him is otherness. He lets those beings speak for themselves. Man's fundamental religiousness is as invincible as is the strangeness itself of other beings. In other words, men is *not* areligious.

This means that areligiousness, as the negation of fundamental religiousness, is possible only as an estrangement of man. Someone is areligious if he views himself as the absolute norm of everything and disregards invincible strangeness. For in this way he cuts himself off from the otherness of beings, including the otherness disclosing itself in his own being. Areligiousness is, therefore, an alienation in the proper sense, one of the second kind we have named. The areligious man belongs to the category of the rebel. Understood in their fundamental sense, then, religiousness and areligiousness are defined here as a relationship to the above-mentioned "strangeness," a relationship of, respectively, openness and closedness.

But, one will object, isn't this a peculiar and arbitrary definition? In reply, let's first consider that such a description is not foreign to a Christian tradition going back as far as Augustine. Thomas Aquinas in particular may be mentioned here. Aquinas starts, of course, from the conviction that man has been created by God, and that's why he begins with religiousness in the full sense, while we are proceeding from the opposite direction. But from religiousness in the full sense Aquinas argues back to something like a fundamental religiousness. Full religiousness for him means a life in union with God, but he also shows that such a life presupposes a condition, viz., that man is receptive, open to God (*capax Dei*).

The receptive man as such doesn't yet recognize God. At first, God's presence is anonymous. He is encountered as a stranger. This happens when the man who doesn't yet recognize God does everything in his power to perfect himself. Such a self-perfecting is only possible if man is faithful to the openness characterizing him as man. Openness to what? To the other than self; man must obtain his perfection from without, he is perfected by the good which, as

Aristotle says, "lies in things," in reality. That's why the soul tends to "the reality existing outside itself." In other words, receptivity for God is a receptivity for the other than self. And this receptivity for the other than self is what we have described as openness for the strangeness which characterizes beings in their intensity and which man himself also retains with respect to himself. This openness is fundamental religiousness.

Secondly, it could be pointed out that our definition more or less imposes itself of necessity. To see this, let us return to the *cogito*, not, however, as it operated in Descartes' philosophy, but as it affected the subsequent history of philosophy. Let us assume that, like Hegel, I concentrate on the first aspect of the *cogito*, the certainty that I am thinking and that therefore I am. I then know that my certainty is so absolute that it cannot even be put in doubt by God. Whether God exists or not makes no difference so far as my certainty is concerned. Thus this certainty implies at least an indifference to the divine. Actually we must say more than this. For we can readily conclude that a certainty which no God can contradict is no longer finite. Such a certainty is itself divine. And that's why the world and everything in it must find their center of reference in this absolute ground.

The man who disregards the invincible strangeness and makes himself the measure of all things is, we said, areligious. This means that such a man, indifferent to God, deifies himself. On the other hand, the man who knows that he is "measured" by the strangeness we have mentioned is religious in the fundamental sense. For he refuses to deify himself, and in doing this he keeps open the question about God.

After these considerations of fundamental religiousness, we must ask again about the problem of secularization. The process of secularization, we said, is the increasing removal of God from the world. Now, as we saw above, the world belongs to man in its entire *extension*. This means that God must be removed from this domain. There is nothing there that can serve as a last foothold for God. In this respect, then, secularization is a process of purification. God's removal from the extension of the world purifies us from the faulty view that God and man are on the same level, competing for a piece of the world. The world, however, has not only an extension but also an *intensity*, an invincible strangeness. One who doesn't disregard this strangeness is religious in this sense that he remains open to otherness and therefore receptive to God, even though God's existence is perhaps a question which he hasn't yet managed to answer.

This means that only now we are in a position where we can correctly formulate the problem of secularization. The often-heard complaint is that modern man seems no longer to be open to God in any way whatsoever. This complaint finds expression in Bonhoeffer's saying that people are so quickly and unashamedly at home in the world. The man who has come of age is at home in the world. If he is there "unashamedly" at home, that is, if he feels that nothing in the world is alien to him and beyond his control, then he neglects the second dimension, that of intensity.

Can something else still be added to this by philosophy? In our opinion, Heidegger can teach us much in this matter. With him we could consider that we live in an era of history that is approaching its climax, viz., the era of calculative thinking, and that the approach of this climax signals the moment when salvation is at hand. Our critique of Hegel's interpretation of history gives us confidence that history doesn't run its course as an evermore consistent development of what has already been thought of. On the contrary, to interpret is to think that which has not yet been thought of.

That's why interpretation gives us in principle a possibility of "reversal," of a "revolutionary" breakthrough which opens up a new direction in what had already been established. It could very well happen that man will again become sensitive to the things that resist conceptual thinking and which can never become fully transparent. It can happen that man will then abandon his aversion to the intensity of the world and that he will become sensitive to the fruitfulness of conflict which, in the final analysis, cannot be conceptualized. It is not impossible that we are approaching the end of that phase of history which is marked with the sign of momentary presence.[12]

---

[12] Cf. p. 68.

There is also a second reason why we have mentioned Heidegger's analysis of modern science. His analysis shows that the scientific-technological world-view of today is not something beyond any further questions. This can prevent us from isolating this world-view from the development from which it came forth, from fixing and absolutizing it. Besides, hermeneutics shows that the objectivity of objectifying science cannot be considered the highest ideal of truth. That's why the principle of verification, as it is used, for instance, by Paul Van Buren, becomes very questionable as soon as one ascribes universal validity to it. Van Buren's hermeneutics hardly deserves its name, for it disregards what interpretation is in the full sense. At most it could be called a hermeneutics of reduction. Such a reductive hermeneutics should not be confused with the kind of hermeneutics defended in this book.

CHAPTER EIGHT

Self-Denial Or Self-Realization?

At the end of the preceding chapter we came close to an important conclusion, but we didn't explicitly formulate it there. One who wishes to offer future man an opportunity to experience the intensity of reality and thereby to experience himself in his fundamental religiousness must recognize those elements of our contemporary history that are empirically non-transparent, resist total conceptual understanding and refer to non-momentary presence. Precisely these elements, however, are rejected by conservative man, for it is among things that can be clearly conceptualized that he feels really at home.

This may seem to be a strange kind of conclusion. Doesn't the conservative present himself precisely as the champion of the eternal values? Doesn't he often play the role of the accuser who indicts others for putting those values in jeopardy? Yet we consider him here as a brake on the development which must give the future man an opportunity to experience his fundamental religiousness.

Let us keep in mind the terminology used in this book, which is concerned with the contrast between the progressive and the conservative man. It stands to reason that not everyone who calls himself—or is called by others—progressive is really progressive. We cannot exclude the possibility that he is a rebel in the sense described in Chapter Six. In other words, the contrast between progressive and conservative is not the same as that between rebel and conservative. Now, with respect to the rebel, who denies that the ego and the others ought to be orientated to the same normativity, the conservative really is the champion of eternal human values. But the other side of the coin is also valid, viz., with respect to progressive man the conservative really acts as a brake on future religiousness.

The intention of this chapter is to clarify the picture of man underlying all our considerations with respect to normative values. We will limit ourselves, moreover, to matters of fundamental ethics. Fundamental ethics has always been centered around the two questions of man's freedom and the norm of freedom. Both of these questions will be seen here in a hermeneutic perspective. For with respect to such an important topic it is of special importance to discover tacit presuppositions. In our opinion these presuppositions are largely the same as those we have met before, in the sense that implicitly a position is taken with respect to individuality. But in the present case this presupposition means that individuality is viewed as identical with ethical untrustworthiness. It is upon this basis that the ethical ideal used to be seen as denial of one's self. Thus we can now say that this chapter is concerned with the truth or falsity of the ideal of self-denial.

1. The Ideal of Self-Denial

Doesn't it go without saying, one may ask, that self-denial is the Christian ideal *par excellence*? Christ called man to deny himself, take up his cross and follow Him. Isn't it pretentious, then, for a Christian to investigate what is true in the ideal of self-denial? One can parry such questions by asking: Isn't man entitled to ask what the term "self-denial" means when Christ calls for self-denial? Now, the Gospel speaks of self-denial in connection with the idea that "he who would save his life will lose it; but he who loses his life for my (Christ's) sake will find it." This idea explains how self-denial should be understood, as is evident from Matthew 16:25, where the call for self-denial is followed by the above quotation, introduced by the particle "for." In other words, self-denial demands that we give up a certain kind of life in order to gain eternal life in Christ.

This, however, means that Christ doesn't call us to destroy our own individuality. On the contrary, we must save ourselves for the life promised by Christ. But under the influence of Platonic philosophy this biblical view of self-denial began to be explained differently even in the first few centuries of Christianity. In the Platonic perspective the ideal of self-denial means that man must renounce everything that is proper to him as this individual man. And this includes his freedom, for freedom makes him an original being, something new and different from all others, it makes him this ego. And so it was assumed that man should deny his own freedom, deny himself "as the ego he is," and that precisely this denial was "self"-denial.

In this chapter we take the term self-denial is this Platonic sense. We intend to show that this view did as a matter of fact arise under the influence of Platonism, in particular that of Plotinus. Next, we will criticize this ideal of self-denial and show how this false ideal contributed to the modern idea that "God is dead" and to the fact that God is no longer heard in the modern world. We will oppose to this ideal of self-denial the ideal of self-realization. Self-realization, we will see, calls to man to renounce the easy path of conformism and invites him to take the difficult road to the ideal. In this way the true content of the biblical ideal of self-denial is safeguarded, at least to the extent that this can be done by philosophy.

Plotinus' picture of man is based on the fundamental distinction between the "inner man" and "the other man." The inner man is "our true self," he is a *soul* that is free of all sensuality and faithful to the intellect. The other man is merely an "image" of the inner man; he is of a lower type, a soul that is connected with the *body* and subject to passions; in short, he is a soul connected with "the animal." Thus we find here Plato's sharp distinction between the intelligible and the sensible; the sensible lies outside the domain of intelligibility. Unsurprisingly, the inner man is eternal and immutable, while the other man is subject to time and change. That's why the ideal for man is that he direct his gaze to the intellect above him.

This is the familiar ideal of *theoria* or contemplation. For only in this way will man ever be able to orientate himself to the principle from which the intellect itself has come forth, to the ineffable origin of everything, which Plotinus calls "the Good" or rather "the One." Man must affirm himself as the inner man. Because of the sharp distinction of the inner man from the other man, this means that he must deny himself as the other man. He must therefore liberate himself from sensuality and the body.

The other man is to a large extent "external" to the inner man. This means, then, that the external must be denied if man is to come to his true self. Everything external is merely "a garment." The man who wishes to be perfect must therefore take off his garments; to be naked means to be pure. After all, the body and the passions are only "additions." That's why Plotinus says: "Take all this away,"[1] take away even the memory of the things of this world. For only then can man become "like unto God"; only when man has stripped himself "of all that" can he strip himself "of everything." Plotinus advises us finally: when you think of the One, give up everything else "so that He alone remains"; do not add anything and ask yourself all the time whether you have really removed everything else from Him. For everything that is not the One is "at the same time both itself and other than itself," but He is "only Himself," "truly Himself," without any admixture of otherness.[2]

This is the ideal of self-denial, that is, the denial of the self living in this world. As we will see, there is a tendency to enlarge this ideal in such a way that it means the denial of the individual self without any qualification. First, however, let us circumscribe the ideal somewhat more in detail. This ideal implies a desocialization of man. It implies that man has already within himself everything needed for his perfection; all he needs to do is give up his orientation to externality. It is true, of course, that many people withdraw into themselves in this way. But in their withdrawal each one of them orientates "himself alone to Him alone."[3] This ideal demands a purification of the passions in the sense that one lays off his passions, and, in addition, this ideal demands the renouncement of every joy that is not one of pure *theoria* or contemplation; hence it

---

1 Plotinus, *Enneades*, V, 3, 17, line 38.
2 *Op. cit.*, VI, 8, 21, lines 25-28.
3 *Op. cit.*, V, 1, 6, line 11.

implies a desexualization. The inner man is not a sexual being. At the same time this ideal is also by definition a denial of the world. Historically it is related to Plato's call to flee from the world in order to become like unto God.

What is the background of this ideal? Man occupies "an intermediary position" between a higher and a lower sphere. The higher sphere is that of the intellect and ultimately that of the One in which any plurality is impossible. Intelligibility is primarily universality. Thus in the sphere of the intellect all of us constitute "a whole." This assertion gives rise to the suspicion that individuality is less good, even evil and ethically unreliable. Is it true that such an under-evaluation of individuality really lies at the basis of the ideal of self-denial? This question must, we think, be answered in the affirmative.

For the present, however, this is merely a suspicion, not yet a certainty. Moreover, there seem to be reasons why the correctness of this suspicion should be doubted. Plotinus himself seems to contradict it. For he says that there are many souls and that their plurality precedes their bond with bodiliness. But if, independently of external "additions," they are many, then they are many on the level of their own high value. How, then, could plurality be a lesser good? Let us see exactly what Plotinus says. The souls, he argues, *must* be many, for the soul comes forth from the intellect, and there are many intellects. The intellects are many because there *must* be differences in the intellect.[4] And if we ask why there must be differences in the intellect, his answer is: because everything which comes forth from the One is not the One, is lower than the One and therefore *must* have "otherness" or non-identity within itself. The One alone hasn't any otherness within itself.

It is precisely this position of Plotinus that demands reflection. To begin with, we must conclude that for Plotinus individuality really is less good than universality. In his philosophy that which is closer to the One is of necessity better that what is farther removed from the One. Now closer to the One is that which is more one and less many; therefore, universality is better than the multiplication of the universal content in individuals. Plotinus would certainly

---

4 *Op. cit.*, IV, 8, 3, lines 6-13 and VI, 2, 22, lines 7-23.

agree with this. In a certain passage of his work he starts with
Socrates as this individual living here on earth and points out that
it would be a mistake to consider this Socrates as the real Socrates,
just as it would be a mistake to address a portrait of Socrates as if it
were Socrates himself. In other words, the Socrates living on earth
is only an image of the intelligible Socrates; and the latter is the
real Socrates. Regarding the relationship between the intelligible
Socrates and the intelligible man in general, it would be wrong to
consider the intelligible Socrates as the intelligible man, for the
intelligible Socrates is evidently only an image of the intelligible
man. These two are related in the same way as the earthly and the
intelligible Socrates. Accordingly, the intelligible man is more true
than the intelligible Socrates, more true than any intelligible individual whosoever; in short, the intelligible man is the "most true."[5]

Secondly, let us try the hypothesis that individuality functionally
possesses a positive significance. The attempt to do this will show
that this hypothesis is not tenable. The soul has two functions
according to Plotinus. It comes forth from the intellect and therefore is cognitive. But the soul is not the intellect and has a specific
function of its own, which is to govern. The question, then, is
whether individuality exercises a positive influence in at least one
of these two functions. But with respect to the function of thinking
individuality cannot exercise any positive influence. As we saw in
Chapters Four and Five, the ego is a source of authentic truth as a
unique and unrepeatable perspective on the one norm. But Plotinus
could not come to such an insight because perspectivity is connected with one's situation, which itself is connected with the body and
the world, while both of these are for Plotinus "additions" from
which the inner man must purify himself. This leaves the second
possibility, viz., that the soul exercises its governing function in an
individual-positive way. Let us examine this possibility.

It doesn't surprise us to hear from Plotinus that the governing
function does not primarily belong to the individual soul but to the
universal soul. From this primary soul the material world came
forth, for every nature necessarily produces what comes after it.
Because the soul is the lower limit at which the light of the
intellect still shines, matter itself must be darkness. But darkness is

_____
[5] *Op. cit.*, VI, 3, 15, lines 30-37.

pure negativity; darkness can only exist and be spoken of in opposition to light. Now, the universal soul is a light; the images of the intellect which it carries in its bosom shine in the darkness. This, then, is the origin of matter. And the universal soul exercises its governing function insofar as the light of its knowledge gives rise to an effect.

The universal soul exercises this function effortlessly and innocently. It remains in the intelligible world and doesn't descend into the material world, so that it isn't affected by darkness. But precisely for this reason the individual souls must remain *united* with the universal soul. That's why they must extend their governing function to the entire material world, without being especially interested in any particular part of this world. Only in this way do they escape suffering and guilt. "They must remain unharmed together with the soul of the totality in the intelligible sphere, exercise government in heaven together with the whole soul, like kings who, in union with the king of the universe, share in the government without themselves descending from the royal palace. Then they are all together in the same place."[6] In other words, there is no question of governing in an individual-positive way.

Moreover, in the lines following this passage it becomes evident that any individual way of governing is the effect of an individual fault, a "sin." "They change," says Plotinus, "and go from the whole to the part; they wish to be themselves and get tired of being together with someone else; and each one withdraws to his own." This apparently happens at a critical moment. The individual souls wish a kingdom of their own; they orientate themselves to their ownness, so that the universality is lost. Elsewhere Plotinus adds that this attitude is one of recklessness (*tolma*).[7]

For Plotinus sin is evidently involved in this; joy over one's ownness and the desire for independence is reckless and insolent. Individual ownness is not something positive but ethically negative. It must be granted that it is indeed not right to affirm one's ownness in such a way that one disregards the unity of norm for all. To do such a thing is what we have called rebellion and reading into a text something that isn't there. This is the element of

[6] *Op. cit.*, IV, 8, 4.
[7] *Op. cit.*, V, 1, 1, line 4.

truth contained in Plotinus' idea. At the same time, however, it appears that Plotinus knows only two of the three possibilities that actually exist. He knows only the acceptance of universality and the affirmation of ownness, conceived in such a way that the one is necessarily at the expense of the other, so that no individual-positive function is possible.

Differently expressed, for Plotinus man can only choose between "belonging to God" and "belonging to himself." It is inconceivable for him that man can be both at the same time. But as soon as man may not affirm his ownness and "belong to himself," the ideal of self-denial tends to extend itself from the denial of the worldly self to the denial of the individual self without any qualification.

A third consideration must be added to this. The soul which in its temerity becomes interested in a particular part of the world establishes itself in the world. Plotinus repeatedly describes how difficult it then becomes for such a soul to remember the intelligible world. The soul increasingly isolates itself from the universal; its contact with the particular piece of the world in which it is interested as its special domain becomes ever more intense. That's why such a soul becomes more and more immersed in matter. The body and the world become ever more the prison and the grave of its innocence. Such a soul is like a captain who in his excessive attachment to his ship perishes together with it. In short, the material world doesn't do the soul any good.

How should this be understood? Let us begin by noting that Plotinus reacts against the gnostics and therefore denies that the material world is evil in itself. For in final analysis this world is a product of the One and the Good. At the same time, however, we should not forget that the material world is the *last* product of the Good, maximally distant from the Good. That's why matter possesses only the absolute minimum of reality, is absolute negativity. Even absolute negativity is not evil in itself. But this doesn't mean that the soul doesn't commit evil by establishing itself in this lowest of all reality. Matter which is not an evil in itself calls forth ethical evil in the soul.[8] That's why the soul must not establish itself in

---

[8] Cf. J. M. Rist, *Plotinus, the Road to Reality*, Cambridge U. Press, 1967, Chapter Nine.

this world. It mustn't seek a domain of its own, it mustn't wish to be independent. The soul must remain where it belongs, that is, in absolute union with the universal soul. It must therefore continue to extend its governing function to the entire material world, without becoming interested in any particular part of it as its own domain.

These three considerations are not unrelated. Let us start with matter which is not evil in itself but which, as pure negativity, calls forth evil effects in the soul which really occupies a higher rank. The individual soul ranks lower than the universal soul. It is not related to the universal soul in absolute negativity but in a qualified denial. Now, because the individual soul is a qualified negativity, any individual function which isn't exercised in absolute union with the universal soul is a function calling forth evil effects in that soul itself. To function individually in the realm of knowing or governing is to function on a lower level than one ought to do. Now, in the soul everything that is lower than it ought to be is ethically evil.

This point is significant for our analysis of self-denial. Self-denial calls primarily for the denial of the self living in the world but secondarily for the denial of the individual self insofar as the latter is not absolutely united to the universal self. In addition, self-denial calls even more loudly for desocialization, desexualization and stripping oneself of the world. The ideal of self-denial is, in final analysis, based on the assumption that the individual is nothing but an arbitrary and interchangeable sample of the species, a sample which has a negative relationship to the fullness of its species and which therefore commits ethical evil if it appeals to its individuality.

Accordingly, this ideal is not adapted to the full meaning of individuality, the meaning in which individuality is equated with non-interchangeable ownness, originality and newness. In other words, that ideal is based on the *logical* primacy of the universal and disregards the fact that in the *ontological* order the primacy doesn't belong to the universal but to the individual. For the individual is the only thing that really *is*.

2. The Many Amendments

It would be disconcerting if one were to dismiss this analysis with the remark that it applies solely to Plotinus and neo-Platonism, for its scope is much wider. Much more is at stake than the influence exercised by Plotinus on medieval thought. The important point is that the fundamental conviction disclosed in the preceding analysis underlies also Aristotelianism and the enormous influence it has exercised on subsequent thinking. While the opposition between Platonism and Aristotelianism is undoubtedly important, it is appropriate to remember here that their disagreement is much less important than their agreement. Their agreement lies in their ideal of *theoria,* their thinking about fixed essences in terms of universal predicates, the ideal of transparency which rejects all opaqueness as negative. But this agreement can be discovered only by one who himself has abandoned the ideal of *theoria.* The following considerations are offered to make this assertion somewhat palatable. The author realizes that they are wholly inadequate as a historical demonstration and presents them only to indicate a certain direction to the interested reader.

In Chapter Six we saw that Augustine saw himself forced to reject all earthly happiness as an alienation from the heavenly fatherland. Precisely in this point he was influenced by Plotinus. The individual soul *must* address itself to the lower in order to govern it, together with the universal soul. This is a necessity and not yet an evil. But the individual soul *may not* do this with too much joy, "with too good a grace."[9] By such a joy the individual soul would isolate itself from the universal soul; hence that joy is sinful. Plotinus explicitly says also that the individual soul gets into difficulties as soon as it "rejoyces over its own freedom."[10] The only permissible joy is the joy of contemplation. But any loving attention to a particular part of the world is in this perspective a "sinful" love, a "worldly" love. We merely may "make use" of the world. This is the fundamental agreement between Plotinus and Augustine.

---

[9] Rist, *op. cit.,* p. 122.
[10] Plotinus, *op. cit.,* V, 1, 1, line 5.

The difference between them consists in this that Plotinus accepts the pre-existence of the soul while Augustine explicitly rejects it. Yet, as we have seen, Plotinus' fundamental idea remains present in a faulty interpretation of the Christian idea of creation. This example is symptomatic for the attitude of the Christian thinkers of the Middle Ages. When a Greek view was too obviously against their faith, these thinkers rejected it, but they failed to recognize the proper character of the Greek sphere of thought. To put it in a nutshell, they introduced many amendments in a faulty plan whose deficiency they couldn't see because they continued to think in terms of the same ideal of *theoria*. These amendments became increasingly more numerous all the time.

It certainly isn't true that Platonism was the predominant philosophy of the Middle Ages. After many centuries of Platonic predominance, Aristotelianism became the established way of thinking in the West. But even then Platonic viewpoints easily managed to maintain themselves in Christian preaching and praxis. The reason is that Aristotelianism itself is an amendment of Platonism, particularly with respect to the central issue of individuality. It is undoubtedly true that Aristotelianism fostered a better view of the unity of body and soul and to some extent also a better view of the unity of human knowledge. One can say that Aristotelianism was responsible for a better understanding of the unity of "man." But "man" is not yet the "individual" man. In Aristotelianism the principle of individuation lies in matter. Now, Aristotelian matter admittedly is not the same as the matter of Plotinus. For Plotinus matter is absolute negativity, but Aristotle expresses himself in a more differentiated way. For him matter is both the absolute negation of every form or content and the inner affirmation of a potentiality, of a real orientation to form and content.

Important as this difference may be, it is no more than an amendment. For matter is orientated to form and content in its totality, so that it is *nothing but* this orientation. In this way the primacy of form and content is re-affirmed. The primacy continues to belong to the universal content, so that individuality doesn't contribute anything new or original to the universal content. Thus the individual must be defined in terms of a certain negativity vis-à-vis the fullness and goodness of the universal content. For

Aristotle also matter is an opaque darkness; he uses the same adjective (*amudron*) as Plato and Plotinus. This opaqueness, says Aristotle, must be "overcome." The clarity of the universal form must throw an ever stronger light on this darkness.[11]

Accordingly, in Aristotelianism also it is unthinkable that the individual can have an individual-positive function with respect to knowing or governing. The individual's task merely is one of adapting himself to the demands of his universal nature. Any independence with respect to these demands must be called, in Plotinus' words, isolation, temerity and sin. This idea also forms the background of the scholastic theory of the natural law. This theory falls within the ideal of self-denial because it takes over the Platonic-Aristotelian under-evaluation of the individual. It calls man to denial of the individual self insofar as this self is not absolutely at one with the universal self. This theory of the natural law also knows only the choice of Plotinus: either acceptance of a universal norm or affirmation of one's ownness. And the choice of the one is necessarily at the expense of the other. In our terminology this choice means either conformism or rebellion. But, as we saw, conformism and rebellion are the two primary forms of estrangement.

The element of truth contained in the above-described position is that the existence of a common norm for the individual must be defended. That's why absolute rebellion, which denies such a common norm, is even more estranging than conformism. Rebellion is indeed the second form of real alienation. The common norm must be saved. But it can be saved only by the one who at the same time affirms his ownness, as we saw—convincingly I hope—in Chapters Four and Five. For the common norm demands to be personally interpreted by the individual who submits to it.

3. Self-Realization in Hegel and Nietzsche

Our temerity in opposing another ideal to the "Christian" ideal of self-denial becomes even more hazardous if this other ideal is introduced with a reference to Hegel and Nietzsche, for Hegel is the

---

11 Aristotle, e.g., *Meteorologica*, bk. 4, ch. 1, 378b 31; *De generatione animalium*, bk. 4, ch. 1, 766b 15, and ch. 4, 770b 16-17.

man who was partly responsible for Nazi totalitarianism, and Nietzsche is well-known as the enemy of Christian morality. As we saw, however, the ideal of self-denial goes back to Aristotle and Plotinus, and we should be careful not to accept benevolently as pre-Christian those thinkers who lived before the Christian era and to reject as "post-Christian" those who came after Christ. The benevolence shown to Aristotle and Plotinus, in the final analysis, merely bears witness to the powers of assimilation possessed by the ancient and medieval Church.

In the chapter about alienation we described how the idea of self-realization derived its impetus from the French Revolution. At the same time, we mentioned that Hegel's philosophy had to be one of self-realization. The emphasis in that chapter fell upon the necessity of alienation, but here alienation is again placed within the context of the entire process of self-realization.

"The progress of the Spirit is development."[12] The absolute Spirit is in development toward an absolute goal. A goal, however, is present from the beginning. This means that the phase of development stands between a beginning and an end which coincide as the poles of the Spirit and which differ as the undeveloped and the developed. The process of development, then, is a "bringing of oneself to oneself,"[13] and therefore a call for absolute freedom since "being with oneself" is freedom according to Hegel. This process is a necessary process. For, as the Absolute, the Spirit is its own cause and necessary; hence everything that is needed for the realization of the absolute freedom of the Spirit is necessary. But being with oneself means recognizing oneself in everything which at first opposes itself to the Spirit as an alien power. This means therefore, that otherness and estrangement are necessary.

Self-realization, then, is self-liberation through self-recognition. The goal of the Spirit is "to make itself and to become for itself the one whom it is in itself,"[14] to be in truth what it is still only in incomplete truth. Self-realization implies the establishment of the truth about oneself. And this self-liberation "in which [the Spirit] goes forward to coming to itself and to realizing its truth," is

---

12 Hegel, *Enzyklopädie,* par. 442.
13 Hegel, *op. cit.,* par. 387.
14 Hegel, *op. cit.,* par. 387.

the "highest and absolute right,"[15] so that everything which is not in line with this development is without right.

What, then, is for Hegel the position to which the finite and individual is by right entitled? It is precisely finiteness itself which, in its limitation, sets foreign boundaries to consciousness. The finite and individual can derive rights only from its development. It *must* develop under penalty of otherwise contradicting itself. One can claim, of course, that the finite must limit itself to its finiteness and the infinite to its infinity. But such a claim is a contradiction, says Hegel, for it imposes a limit on the infinite. And if, on the other hand, one limits the finite to its finiteness, one establishes the finite as something that is ultimately fixed, thereby absolutizing it. Accordingly, infinity and finiteness, taken in isolation, have no truth. Only the totality which has transcended all opposition is true. In particular, the finite, divorced from "the totality," has no truth. Thus the truth of the finite reveals itself as a "going beyond and transcending of itself."

How the individual transcends himself becomes most manifest in the activity by which he produces a work. When he still has only an incomplete truth about himself, the individual does not think that he produces a work in order to transcend himself but only in order to express himself. But he must come to the realization that all other individuals are interested in his work, just as he is interested in theirs, and that he deceives himself when first he says that his work interests him only because it is his work and then that he is disinterestedly orientated to his work as *a* work. From this it follows that the work is common to all, that it is "the work of all and of each." When he realizes this, the individual reaches the sphere of the spiritual, which is precisely the sphere of all and of each. He then ceases to resist the other individuals and transcends himself toward his truth, viz., the universal and the spiritual.

In short, in a self-transcending movement the individual must become what he is—an incomplete spirit who must strip himself of his incompleteness. Then the Spirit becomes individual, even as individuality becomes universal. This insight is created in us by the

---

15 Hegel, *op. cit.*, par. 550.

Spirit "who calls to all consciousness: 'Be for yourselves what all of you are in yourselves—rational.' "[16]

In Hegel we find the elements that are of essential importance for a philosophy of self-realization. First of all, self-realization is a self-liberation and self-recognition in which one goes forward to encounter the truth about oneself, and this self-realization implies a confrontation with otherness and strangeness. Secondly, man is described as a "transcending of himself." Thirdly, this process is inevitable and necessary. But this doesn't mean that one cannot frustrate it. Resistance, however, to the inescapable development is possible only as an estrangement, that is, a negative estrangement.

But in Hegel all these elements are presented within the framework of his philosophy of the Spirit. The critique we have thus far exercised on Hegel's approach focused on his failure to see that individuality, otherness and strangeness—and therefore also history—cannot be transcended because beings remain foreign to me in their intensity and because the individual has priority over the universal and the species. Now, it is certain that Hegel included under the universal also the element of normativity. But this means normativity at the expense of ownness or ownness at the expense of normativity. The truth of this assertion shows itself, for instance, when Hegel speaks of work. It is true that the work possesses a kind of autonomy and that, as the expression of its maker's individuality, it is incompletely and only psychologically interpreted. Work, as the bringing into language of truth, is indeed, "of all and of each." But it is not true that therefore we reach here a domain where the individuals cease to be opposed to one another. For if the truth of the work is not to sink away in foreignness, each one must understand it in his own way and consequently in an ever-different way. The preservation and completion of the truth of the work demands that each one's ownness be brought to bear on it and, consequently, that this ownness be preserved.[17]

Hegel's philosophy has a strangely Plotinian character. Like Plotinus, it is a philosophy of the total home-coming and the return.

16 Hegel, *Phänomenologie des Geistes*, Glockner ed., p. 414.
17 Cf. p. 38.

Moreover, to the extent that the Spirit has an existence apart from human spirits—a point that remains uncertain in Hegel—it is also a philosophy of the pure beginning, which re-inforces its character as a return to home. This leads to the paradoxical conclusion that the Spirit realizes itself while the individual man is offered the Plotinian ideal of self-denial.

Yet this is the case. The individual, says Hegel, must "transcend himself," but this means he must transcend himself toward the domain of the "rational" in which all individuals are "equivalent to one another." The Spirit's self-realization is, with respect to individual objects, a process in which they are deobjectified and re-absorbed into subjectivity, and with respect to individual subjects a process in which they are universalized. There is no room here for an individual-positive function in knowledge or governing. The individual remains subject to the classical suspicion of ethical unreliability. That's why obedience, as "obedience to the law and to the legal institutions of the State" is for Hegel "authentic freedom."[18]

In Hegel the individual's self-denial is encompassed by the framework of the self-realization of the absolute Spirit and becomes the victim of this. We can now see another tendency in the ideal of self-denial. One doesn't go far enough by saying that the good man must sacrifice himself. Man does not sacrifice himself *to* God, but is a victim *of* God. God demands of man that he be good. Within the context of the above-described ideal this means that God demands the elimination of individual ownness. This idea applies not only, as we have seen, to Platonism but wherever the affirmation of ownness is conceived as falling short of the universal normativity; in other words, also when the universal natural law is conceived as the *highest* moral norm.

In such a view obedience becomes the highest virtue, at least when obedience is understood as it appears here, that is, as the disregarding of ownness. The inner tendency of this kind of obedience is appropriately expressed in the idea that one must obey "as a corpse." Anything the individual has in living autonomy must be sacrificed to God. The God who makes such a demand, however, is a very primitive god, a jealous god, who cannot bear man's autono-

---

18 Hegel, *Enzyclopädie*, par. 552.

my. This idea of God is contained in Plotinus' view of "temerity" (*tolma*).

Individual ownness, however, is something given to man by the Creator-God. By demanding that man be "good," a jealous God would overrule his own work of creation. He thereby would resemble the old god Chronos who devoured his own children. Chronos is the time-god; the man who lives in time must be devoured. In this view temporality is understood in an exclusively negative way. It is not a productive power but marked with the sign of loss. The underlying idea evidently is that either at the beginning of time or at a particular moment in time there was a fullness with respect to which all further time can only be a loss. This loss must be prevented by preserving unchanged the fullness that is posited as present. The most radical way of doing this is to eliminate all subsequent time. This is a logical implication of any philosophy of "return." Within its perspective the idea of something like "revelation" can only be understood as an event that *has* taken place in an absolutely *closed* past. God *has* spoken; He speaks no longer and will not speak again. That's why He demands the elimination of all time after He has spoken.

The new ideal of self-realization is present in Hegel, but only in favor of the absolute Spirit. The ideal remains deficient because Hegel's image of man remains defective. Hence what the ideal of man's self-realization will be can disclose itself only when our thinking takes seriously the idea that man is entitled to his individual ownness. As we have pointed out in Chapter Three, Husserl assigned this right to the individual. But the problematics called up by Husserl demands a hermeneutic. That's why the new ideal will manifest itself only in the hermeneutical perspective. A few features of this new ideal, however, manifested themselves long before Husserl. We may refer to the young Nietzsche, who in one of his meditations assigns an ideal of his own to the individual.

When a traveller who had visited many countries, so Nietzsche relates, was asked which human characteristic he had seen everywhere, he answered: laziness. Shouldn't he have said: the fact that all people are afraid? For they hide behind customs and opinions.

"Fundamentally every man knows very well that he is only once, as something unique, in the world" and that no chance, rare as it may be, can ever give rise to this man a second time. Man knows this, but he hides this as a bad conscience. Why? Because he is afraid of his neighbor, who demands that one behave according to conventions and who himself hides behind these conventions. But why does man fear his neighbor and live as one of the herd, without rejoycing that he is himself? The usual reason is that he is lazy. The traveller was right: people are more lazy than afraid.

What they fear most of all is the many difficulties which they would encounter if they wished to be unconditionally honest and stand naked before themselves. Only artists hate the established modes of behavior and the traditional views; that's why they reveal everyone's bad conscience, "the statement that every man is a unique miracle." They have the courage to show us man as he is, in everyone of his muscular movements, himself, himself alone, beautiful and remarkable in the rigid consistency of his uniqueness, new and unbelievable, and not at all boring. The great thinker who despises people despises their laziness which makes them appear as uniform factory products. One who doesn't wish to be part of the herd must cease to make it easy for himself. He must follow his conscience, which tells him: "Be your self. What you do, think and desire now—all this is not what you are."

Every young human being hears this call and trembles. For if he thinks of his true liberation, he begins to have an inkling of the happiness that is awaiting him from all eternity. But he will never attain this happiness as long as he is chained by fear. And how desolate, how meaningless life can become without liberation! Nature doesn't know any being more repulsive than the man who has fled from his own genius. Such a man can no longer be seized, for he is wholly externalized and bereft of any core. And if a lazy man is said to kill time, then we must say of a period in which people surrender to their own laziness that it really will be killed, that is, that it will be removed from the history of true liberation.

We must be encouraged to live according to our own standard and our own law, especially because we live *now*. For, strange as it is, we live just now although we have had infinite time to come to be. We possess nothing but this brief time of today and in this short time we must show why we have come to be just now. We must render account for our existence. We wish to take the direction of our life into our own hands. "I am going to try to become free," says the young man. Must this plan be prevented because two nations happen to be at war with each other, or because two continents of the earth are separated by an ocean, or because a religion is taught which didn't yet exist two thousand years ago? "All this is not what you are," the young man tells himself. "No one can build the bridge by which you must cross life, no one but you yourself. There are, of course, numerous paths and bridges and half-gods who wish to help you with the crossing, but at the expense of yourself; you would mortgage and lose yourself. In this world there is one solitary road which no one but you can go. Where does it lead? Do not ask such a question, but simply take this road."

How can man learn to know himself? Man is something dark and hidden. Were he to have seven times seventy layers and were he to peel off all of them, he still would not be able to say: this is no longer a peel but the very core. It isn't necessary, however, to descend so laboriously into the shaft of one's own essence. For everything bears witness to our essence—our friendships and own enmities, our look and our handshake, what we remember and what we forget, our books and our writing. The young man, then, has a means at his disposal. He must look back over his life and ask himself: what have you really loved thus far? The things you respect and love will perhaps give you a law, "the fundamental law of your own self."

You should, therefore, investigate how your various interests supplement and surpass one another, how they explain each other. They constitute the ladder by which thus far you have climbed up toward yourself. "For your true essence does not lie concealed deep in you but immeasurably high above you, or at least above that which you usually consider your self." Ask yourself in particular which educators and which examples really spoke to you. Your own "primordial meaning" (*Ursinn*) will then become clear to you; you will see your own core "which cannot be educated and formed and which is difficult to approach, tied up and paralyzed." That's why your educators are really your liberators."[19]

The most characteristic difference between Hegel and Nietzsche is that Nietzsche assigns to man a truly individual ideal. While Hegel calls upon the individual to become "rational" and enter the domain where all individuals are "equivalent to one another," Nietzsche appeals to him to be himself in such a way that he is not like the others. The characteristics, however, which accompanied the self-realization of the absolute Spirit occur also in Nietzsche's ideal. Here also self-realization is a self-liberation and self-liberation implies a self-recognition in the objects of one's own interest and love. My love alone obviously bears witness here to the truth of my life, so that self-realization is growing in my truth.

And the idea that man is a "transcending of himself" assumes in Nietzsche the more purified form of not transcending one's individuality but one's ordinary self that is determined by others. Plotinus could agree with Nietzsche that man ascends higher, but in opposition to Plotinus and Hegel man's ascent is localized by Nietzsche within the individual self. I ascend to the height of my self.

Finally we find in Nietzsche also the necessity which characterizes the process of self-realization. True, the self can back away from self-realization, but he then lapses into self-alienation; his life becomes a life which lets slip by the happiness awaiting it from all eternity, a desolate, meaningless and repulsive life, a life that has become all exteriority and bereft of any core. Of such an estranged life one can say that it runs its course in time but that the time of this life has not become history and therefore should be destroyed.

Nietzsche expresses the necessity of self-realization by several terms: "height," but more especially by "standard," "fundamental law" and "primordial meaning" (Ursinn). Every life has a law of its own. The fact that this law applies only to me, in such a way that I must take a road not assigned to anyone else, doesn't take away its character of a law. My law is not subject to my freedom. The statement that man is free means first and foremost that he is able to look for his own law. This law itself is "not subject to education."

---

[19] Nietzsche, "Unzeitgemässe Betrachtungen," drittes Stück, in the Schlechta ed. of Nietzsche's Werke, vol. 1, pp. 287-290.

The statement that man is subject to education means precisely that education can set man free to go forward to his "uneducable" self. My law, Nietzsche adds, is "tied" and "paralyzed." What he means by "tied" is, we think, that this law is not subject to my fancy; but what does he mean by calling it "paralyzed"? Perhaps he wishes to convey that my ordinary self can flee away from the demands of my higher self, but that my higher self cannot flee; without ever changing its location, my higher self calls upon my ordinary self to become this higher self.

4. The Authentic Self As Ethical Norm

In the preceding pages we have opposed the new ideal of self-realization to self-denial. But self-realization presents itself as a self-liberation. A suspicion arises here that self-realization and self-denial do not share a common notion of freedom. Let us see which presuppositions these two have about freedom.

The classical conception of freedom was established by scholastic philosophy. It points out that man has the possibility to accept any particular object which attracts him because it is attractive or to reject it in spite of its attractiveness, or even that man has the power to take or not to take any position with respect to such an object. This power is based on the very essence of the rational striving which willing is. For willing is consequent upon rational knowing. Just as rational knowledge is orientated to the true as true, so rational tending is orientated to the good as good. Now the good as good is to some extent realized in any particular object and this is the reason why the rational striving is able to accept the particular object. But the particular object is never the total realization of the good as good; it is only relatively good; that's why the rational striving is not necessitated by it and remains capable of rejecting it as only relatively good. Even the taking of a position with respect to the particular object is only a particular good; for this reason the rational striving is free to take or not to take a position in reference to the particular object.[20]

What are the characteristics of this theory of freedom? Without denying that the theory has undergone many subsequent amend-

---

[20] J. Peters, *Metaphysics*, Pittsburgh, 1963, pp. 323 ff.

ments, one must still say, we think, that freedom is fundamentally seen as a freedom of choice. As such, its primary role is concerned with the particular act, first with this particular act, then that particular act and all other particular acts, each one of them *taken separately.*

Secondly, this theory is based on the primacy of the intellect at the expense of the movement of self-transcendence. These two aspects of the theory re-inforce each other; the theory pays attention to the separate acts and disregards the historicity of human development.

Thirdly, fellowman plays no role at all in the decision of the free man. The significance of this will become evident when we describe freedom as project.

Finally, we must ask, what is the basis on which this freedom makes its decision? The will, so we are told, is orientated to the good as good, and this is the orientation that is of essential importance here. But the relative good does not fill this orientation; therefore, it is not of necessity included in this necessary orientation. The question, however, is precisely, on what basis is the relative good included when it is included? The reply that man cannot forever continue to deliberate and has to make a decision is not satisfactory, for it does not result in a preference for either acceptance or rejection. To escape this difficulty, defenders of the theory add that man brings his concrete affective inclination to bear on the issue. But they quickly add that even this inclination is not necessitating. And so they conclude that the free man lets himself be determined *by himself*, for this is precisely what freedom is.

We would like to observe here that such an approach makes the free decision wholly unintelligible. The important point is not so much that the free decision becomes unintelligible for other people as that it is also unintelligible for the free man himself. In final analysis, so it appears, man does free acts because he happens to be free. Now it may be true that freedom always retains something unintelligible; nevertheless, it needs to be investigated whether freedom cannot acquire a greater measure of intelligibility than it is given in the description above. The question that needs to be asked is: what does freedom mean for the individual man, for his ownness and his life-history?

Differently expressed, freedom must be viewed not merely as an essential property of man in general but also, and even more so, as something within the individual human being insofar as he differs from all other human beings. The classical conception of freedom failed to do this, so that the individual's free decision remains unintelligible there. Now, insofar as such a decision is motivated from within freedom itself and therefore unintelligible, it reveals itself necessarily as an element of arbitrariness, a "choice" made by "the will." This tacit presupposition gives rise to the desire to bind freedom to a norm which will not allow it any individual-positive function with respect to the norm, viz., the universal norm with which the individual must remain in harmony at the expense of his own self. It is this presupposition about freedom that underlies the ideal of self-denial.

Which conception of freedom is presupposed by the idea of self-realization which is a self-liberation? Let us illustrate the point through an example. I enter a bookshop, where I encounter a student whom I don't know in person but I happen to know that he is one of the victims of a recent cut in student grants. All I know about him is that he must try to make ends meet on a very small stipend. But I am impressed by the fact that I see him there buying a book that is extremely expensive. How would the classical theory of freedom explain this purchase?

The book, it would say, is a fundamental work about the history of art, virtually indispensable and therefore also attractive for this student who majors in the history of art. On the other hand, its purchase cuts deeply into his monthly allowance, and this is not attractive. The student was free, then, but his interest in the history of art weighed heavily; that is to say, he made it weigh heavily, he himself made his interest the motive of his decision. That's all there is to it; no further questions need to be asked.

Let us suppose, however, that I have become curious, talk to the student and that, in spite of my inquisitiveness, a genuine conversation develops. I learn that he has chosen his major study interest with great enthusiasm. He didn't get much help in the realization of his plans, for he comes from an environment in which art and long-haired artists are only spoken of with scorn. Artists don't realize how serious life is, he was told, and most of them are parasytes kept alive by welfare checks. Not that money is everything, of course, but it is very important. Why, then, should he choose such a risky profession when sooner or later he can take over the flourishing enterprise of his father? "Of course, you are free to do whatever you wish," his father told him, "but if you choose art, don't expect any help from me."

From this conversation I acquire a better understanding of the purchase which had impressed me. It remains true that the student in freedom made his interest in the book his motive, as is held by the classical theory of freedom, but I now understand it better. I realize that this young man would have come in contradiction with himself if he had not purchased that book. The particular free act becomes more intelligible against the background of the freedom with which he has chosen his own way of life. But, one could object, doesn't the unintelligibility seem to return here on the deeper level of one's own "choice" of life? Let us not be too hasty in drawing this conclusion, although the question itself is legitimate: why does a human being enter this way of life rather than that?

In the above-given example the answer could be: "I cannot envisage myself as a factory manager," "It would be nothing for me," or "I have other interests." This means that a way of life is chosen because one doesn't wish to be *in contradiction with oneself*. What is typical, moreover, in our example is that the young man is not and has never been a factory manager. Prior to a situation which will never become a fact because he himself prevents it, he knows that he would contradict himself if he allowed that situation to come about. Man evidently is characterized by "being ahead of himself," by anticipating upon himself.

But who is this "self" of which he knows that it is contradicted by the situation of the factory manager and affirmed by the art historian? For in actual fact the student has not yet been an art historian but merely prepares himself to become one. This "self," then, is not the factical ego. One strives precisely to see to it that the situation in which the ego *de facto* is or will be doesn't constitute a contradiction with what the ego authentically is.

Here, again, freedom discloses itself as self-determination. But it can now be described as the possibility to give to one's own life a form that will not lead away from but toward the authentic ego. Freedom is the anticipating project of my authentic ego, in virtue of which I put my facticity more and more at the service of my authenticity. Accordingly, human freedom and self-realization are identical.

Earlier in this work, we didn't say that self-realization is freedom but that it is self-liberation. What, then, is the liberating power of freedom? The answer is that the ego no longer lets itself be determined by the others and, in this sense, liberates itself from them. We will present here a brief sketch of this process of liberation, while reserving a more precise analysis of it for the end of of the chapter.

The little child that is still helpless has to be determined by others. This is an event having a positive value because in this way the child opens himself to the domain of the others. On the basis of this event, however, a true alienation also becomes possible. Its first and most obvious form is the conformism in which the child lets himself be determined by the others. The ego which conforms does not attain self-determination. Metaphorically expressed, the ego lacks a direction of movement of its own and aimlessly wanders around, far from itself. But in this situation it hears a call and discovers its freedom as a possibility to listen to this call.

What is the call of which there is question here? Let us recall that Hegel described his ideal, "Be for yourselves what all of you are in yourselves—rational," as a call, for it is the Spirit who "calls in this way to all consciousness." But the ideal of self-realization has been formulated in a more refined way by Nietzsche. He, too, speaks of a call. The man who no longer wishes to be one of the herd merely has to stop making it easy for himself: "Let him follow his conscience, which calls to him: Be your self. You are not all that which you now do, think or desire."

It is, however, especially Heidegger who has analyzed the character of this call. Heidegger asks four questions in this matter:

1. Who is called? The "I" which understands itself and the world as the anonymous "they" do in everyday life and in an existence that has fallen into inauthenticity.

2. To what is the "I" called? To be its own self. The call, then, disregards everything which the "I" could mean in the eyes of the others and which it wishes to be in their eyes. Hitherto the "I" has established itself in the meaning it has for the others, but the call deprives it of this hiding place. Now the "I" is placed face to face with itself. This doesn't mean that the "I" withdraws from the world, but that now it is confronted with the demand to explain both itself and the world in its own way.

3. What does this call say? Strictly speaking, nothing. The call doesn't contain any communication, it has nothing to say. The self is not told anything but simply called to itself. The call, then, doesn't speak, save in the form of silence. Nevertheless, the call is not ambiguous, for it orientates, it indicates a direction.

4. Finally, who is the one who calls? The caller does not give his name and remains silent about his origin and position. He is wholly bound up in his calling. Shouldn't we say, then, that the "I" calls itself? No, for the "I" that is called is precisely the "I" that lets itself be determined by others; hence this "I" *is* in a different way than the one who calls. The call, we should realize, is not a little plan of our own; it is not prepared by ourselves or willed by ourselves. The call comes against our expectation and even against our will. Similarly, it is certain that the call does not come to us from a fellow-man. "The call comes *from* me and yet *from beyond* me." To conclude *at once* that, therefore, the call comes from God would be disregarding the phenomenon that the call, coming from me yet from beyond me, addresses itself to me. The call belongs primarily to man's own mode of being.[21]

It is in the man who lets himself be determined by the others, the man who wanders around without an orientation of his own, that the call resounds to be himself and to live without coming in contradiction with himself. This call sounds from afar because his self is still far from himself; but from the moment when the call is heard the darkness is pierced, not by light but by a call which

---

[21] Heidegger, *Being and Time*, sect. 56 and 57, pp. 272 ff.

doesn't change its location and therefore can serve as a beacon by which the self can orientate itself.

It is not surprising that the "I" which is thus called is inclined to begin its journey toward the self with rebellion, for the only certainty I have that my orientation is my own is that I am not following the road of others. Rebellion, however, is insufficient; it doesn't show how I am myself. The "I" must also liberate itself from rebellion, for rebellion is only a self-liberation with respect to conformism. In final analysis self-realization is a self-liberation because it puts my facticity on the road to my authentic self; it is a liberation from inauthenticity.

Accordingly, the theme of self-realization has as its center the idea of the authentic self. Let us add a few considerations to clarify what authentic being means.

Terminology. In Chapter Six we spoke of the authentic man. Authenticity, in the sense in which the term was used there, is a quality. But the authentic self of which there is question here is not a quality but the proper being of man. The opposite of authenticity as a quality is inauthenticity, but the opposite of the authentic self as the proper being of man is the facticity of man. Let us add that the two meanings are obviously connected. Authenticity as a quality is precisely the quality of one who has orientated his life to the call coming from his authentic self. In the following pages we use "authentic self" in reference to the proper being of the individual man.

The Authentic Self and Thrownness. How should the one who calls be understood? The one who calls is not the one who is called, says Heidegger, for the latter precisely allows himself to be determined by the others. Thus the called man is not yet what the caller wishes him to be. But how can a call come forth from something that has not yet been realized? In principle, the answer is: because the *de facto* existing reality is not the only reality. In this formula we find the element of truth contained in Platonism. Moreover, the *de facto* existing reality is conceivable only on the basis of another reality, viz., the real possibility.

Now, however, the question returns: with what must the real

possibility of the individual man be connected? For this possibility
cannot be a free-floating possibility, but must be a real possibility of
this man. But who is *this* man? He is the man who is thrown into
this world. The central point of thrownness is that no man has
himself decided that he would be born. Consequently, in no way
could he decide how he would be born, as what kind of a man.
The thrown man finds himself as determined and limited. Thrownness situates man in the dimension of his past. Accordingly, the
statement that the authentic self of this man is not a free-floating
possibility means that his authentic self remains connected with his
limitation and his past.

Authentic Being as Goal and Future. Nevertheless, authentic
being and thrownness do not merge. The authentic self is identical
with the own possibilities contained in the own limitation of this
man. If thrownness expresses the limitation of my possibilities, then
the authentic self expresses the possibilities of my limitation. The
same idea can also be put differently. Thrownness is my past, but
the authentic self is that which prevents my past from ever becoming past in the perfect tense, that is, a past that is closed off. The
past lying behind me demands that I take it up and carry it
forward toward a new future in which it will be perfected in
accordance with the own possibilities which in an unfinished way
were present in the past.

The Necessitating Character of the Authentic Self. It is obvious
that thrownness has a necessitating character; there is no escape
from the fact that I have been thrown into existence as this limited
human being. There is, therefore, also no escape from the fact that
I am circumscribed by the own possibilities of my limitation and
the unfinished character of my possibilities. But it is precisely in
the unfinished character of my possibilities that lies the call addressed to me to become my self by orientating myself toward my
own possibilities. There is no other possibility for one who doesn't
wish to come in contradiction with himself than to take the road of
his own possibilities. This means that the call has a necessitating
character.

The Authentic Self and Freedom. Does freedom remain possible
if the authentic self has a necessitating character? We cannot
escape this difficulty by saying that the authentic self is necessi-

tating on the one condition that man wishes to become his own self. For everyone wishes to become his own self. Nevertheless, the possibility of freedom is not eliminated; on the contrary, it is only now that this possibility discloses itself. Man, we should recall, is threatened by the obvious danger of conformism. Even the man who conforms wishes to become himself, but he thinks, with the laziness mentioned by Nietzsche, that the others can tell him who he is. He thereby lets these others take away his freedom and his movement toward his own authentic self. But if he listens to the call coming forth from his own proper being, he regains both his freedom and his movement toward his authentic self. Liberated from determination by the others, he proceeds from within toward the realization of his own possibilities, which in their unfinished condition call him to bring them to completion.

Freedom as Anticipating Project of the Authentic Self. The fact that man can listen to the call although it calls him toward possibilities that have not yet been realized is due to the anticipating power which human freedom is. Anticipating upon his future, he projects a total picture of himself as the man who he properly is and must become. Because he has such a total picture of himself at his disposal, he is able to decide now and to act. Such an anticipation, however, is necessarily premature and subject to error and sin.

Since Husserl made his analysis of the thing-perception, we know that every anticipation is presumptive. The same presumption is contained in the attitude of the reader who begins to read a text and, after reading a short part of it, bases his expectations from the whole book on the few lines he has read. In a similar way man projects ahead of himself a total meaning as soon as he is confronted with the first lines of the text of his life. Should freedom, then, be accused of acting prematurely? Only if it is not ready to correct its anticipating expectations but fixes and immobilizes them, for it would thereby become estranged from its own essence and decrease its power of anticipation. But if freedom remains faithful to itself, it continues to be the anticipating project which it is and will constantly re-examine and correct its anticipations.

Precisely because a presumption is connected with the anticipation, man must remain ready to revise the anticipated total picture which he has projected of his authentic self according as he makes

progress in reading the text of his life; that is to say, according as
he acts and makes decisions on the basis of his project. For these
actions and decisions either harmonize with the call or are contradicted by it. In this way I get to know that, thus acting and
deciding, I am on the right road or deviate from it. I thereby
acquire a stronger awareness of my authentic self, so that my
revised anticipation can be a purer project of it.

The Authentic Self and Life-time. The revised project, however,
remains a project, a completion of my unfinished possibilities but,
at the same time, always an anticipation upon their realization and,
consequently, no definitive completion. Thrownness, we said, is
never a completed past, that is, it is never closed in such a way
that it doesn't have any longer a future. To this we must now add a
second sense in which the past is never completed: the past can
never be completed in such a way that it will wholly merge into
the future and cease to be past and incomplete. I anticipate my
possibilities totally and, nonetheless, only by approximation and
interpretation; that's why they can be realized only in an approx-
imate way and not exhaustively.

This means that it is meaningful to compare my life-history with
the reading of a text. My authentic self functions as the text to be
read and my freedom as the ego which must interpret the text of
my life. As in the relationship between reader and text, there
occurs here a completion, but it never is the definitive completion.
In both cases also time is hermeneutically fruitful, genuinely productive of truth—with respect to the present case of my life-time,
it is the time in which I more truthfully become the one I ought to
be. All the time and only the time in which I come to be in this
way is my history.

The Authentic Self as "Not Being-at-Home." A text which I have
not yet sufficiently interpreted stands before me in its invincible
otherness. In a similar way my own possibilities, insofar as they
always remain not yet sufficiently interpreted, stand before my
interpreting freedom in their unexpected otherness. To the extent
that I have already interpreted them, they are familiar to me, but
because my interpretation cannot gage them exhaustively, they
always remain more strange than familiar, I remain, in final analysis, a stranger unto myself. In Heidegger's language, my ownmost

possibilities are my "not being at home," the reason why I can never establish myself in myself as my home and even less ever definitively rely on the interpretation given by someone else. In the final chapter we will go beyond Heidegger and consider that precisely this strangeness which I have for myself can constitute the phenomenal starting point of an argument for God's existence.

The Authentic Self Is My Norm. As the text is the norm for my interpretation, so my authentic being is the norm for my self-interpretation. In more traditional terms, freedom is the means by which the authentic self, as the goal anticipated in any interpretation, must be realized. Now, the means refers to the goal; therefore, the means is used in the wrong way if attainment of the goal is prevented. For the authentic self must be realized; in this sense it has a necessitating character. How can freedom be used in the wrong way? This happens when one is powerless or unwilling, and only in the case of being unwilling is there question of guilt. Hermeneutically the ethical fault should be understood in this way. If I turn my freedom against my self-realization, I strip my lifetime of its productive and truth-building character, I undo it as my history, I act as if this time could be eliminated. The ethical fault is the attitude in which I devour my own history.

If everyone is subject to a law of his own, so that everyone ought to live in accordance with his own law, how can there still be a human society? The question is all the more urgent because one's own law doesn't communicate anything, doesn't issue any specific orders, but merely calls upon man. Doesn't such an attitude lead to absolute anarchy? Even the least developed society requires general laws and norms, and this requirement of state and society at large applies also to a community of ethical people. The ethical norm, so the objection goes, doesn't lie in the authentic self but in the *universal human essence,* which unfortunately is often called "the natural law."

The threatening problem of anarchy is a matter which we have met before in Chapter Six, and the answer given there applies here also. Reformulated with respect to the present problem, the answer points out that the man who goes forward to his authentic self does not draw back to refer only to himself. On the contrary, he gives his own interpretation both to himself and to the others. The authentic man introduces the other to his interpretation and thereby delivers him—albeit not exhaustively—from the incompleteness of his truth. The fundamental attitude of the authentic man is love.

But this answer does not suffice with respect to the second question. What is the relationship between the authentic self and the universal essence of man? This is a very delicate question, which needs to be treated in the clearest possible way. We will therefore begin by distinguishing not two but three levels, viz., the authentic self, the universal essence of man and the interpretations in which the content of this universal essence is explained. Because our question is concerned with the first two levels, we may clarify the question by beginning with the third level.

Many contemporary discussions are only concerned with this third level. It is rightly pointed out that the official ecclesiastical interpretations of the human essence are based on a medieval—that is, largely Greek—picture of man. For example, so they argue, those people who constantly use the term "natural law" as a rule interpret human nature too biologically, and this interpretation is connected with the Greek tendency to isolate man's spirit from his corporeity and to understand this corporeity in the perspective of material and animal nature. What is lacking in such considerations is that the crucial point lies in the conception of individuality. It is only when one realizes what standpoint Platonic-Aristotelian philosophy occupies with respect to the individual that one understand the presuppositions underlying various ecclesiastical pronouncements. This book makes an attempt to bare this presupposition and to sketch the development from the Greek to the contemporary picture of man by means of a few central issues.

The different re-interpretations of man's essence make us realize that even general laws expressing the universal essence of man do not arise in a vacuum, but are based on presuppositions, with respect to which it always remains to be seen whether they can still be ours. In this way those re-interpretations prevent man from becoming estranged from himself by accepting the universal law in an interpretation that is not of his time. Moreover, the possibility of collaborating in a contemporary interpretation offers each individual human being an opportunity to live as the interpreting being which he is and to prevent his observing the law in a conformistic way, i.e., without taking any personal attitude.

Let us now return to the first two levels. In other words, we are now no longer concerned with the question whether or not the universal law is interpreted in a contemporary way, with the interpretation of the content of man's universal essence. The only point at issue here is how one's authentic self as norm is related to the universal essence which is traditionally called the norm. Let us first repeat the central idea of this chapter and then outline this idea more accurately, indicating its limitation.

When we repeat the central idea of this chapter, it becomes apparent that the essential decision has already been made. For we have seen that it is a faulty prejudice to think that the authentic self must so absolutely harmonize with the demands of the universal essence that self-denial of authentic being is required in the case of conflict. The statement that man is subject to norms must indeed be maintained, but, in the first place, normativity lies primarily in the authentic self and, in the second place, this normativity can only be safeguarded by the ego's own interpretation; hence the preservation of the normativity demands the preservation of the individual's ownness. This position doesn't lead to the danger of arbitrariness because the authentic ego is, as Heidegger says, not a little plan of freedom but based on a call which often contradicts my expectations. In short, the ego is governed by a law of its own, and freedom is precisely the possibility to fulfill this law.

Although it lies outside the scope of this book, I'd like to add here a psychological remark. As we saw, the anticipations in which freedom gives an interpretation of its authentic self are always premature. But, in addition to being premature, they are also partly wrong, as is clear from the comparison with the hermeneutical model. However, the continued reading of a text brings the faulty prejudices to light because they impede the understanding of the text in such a way that the text becomes unintelligible, thereby creating a situation in which I proceed to revise my prejudices. On the other hand, as Freud has shown, man can create resistances in himself which prevent him from recognizing the faulty character of his prejudices about himself. These resistances

can be so strong that they almost deprive life of all meaning; yet
even then it can happen that man fails to recognize his prejudices
as false. Even when they are less strong, they continue to operate
in a negative way as a violation of the purity of one's self-
interpretation. Accordingly, the clear understanding of the authentic self is not a simple affair.

In principle, however, it remains evident that my authentic self
is my total norm, a norm that is proportionate to me. With respect
to this proportionate norm the universal human essence is a *reduced* norm, for it doesn't express my unrepeatable ownness, being
based as it is on the tacit assumption that individuals are interchangeable and alike.

At this stage, however, the limitation by which the truth of this
idea will be more accurately situated begins to make itself felt.
What makes us suspect that there is a limitation? The universal
human essence, we said, is a reduced norm because it assumes that
everyone is like everyone else. In its sweeping character this assumption is wrong, but isn't it true that to a considerable degree
every human being is alike? The position taken in this book is that
the individual has a priority over the species, which means that he
may not be subordinated to the species. But it should not be taken
to mean that the individual doesn't belong to the species.

A second reason to suspect that a restriction must be made is
concerned with obedience. Obedience, the reader will recall, was
described as the denial of one's ownness in favor of the universal
normativity. Such an obedience undoubtedly is not adapted to the
authentic being of the self, especially because the authentic self
speaks only in the form of silence, as a call indicating a direction of
movement, which as such does not issue any specific order that I
could obey. Nevertheless, isn't it possible to conceive phases of life
and situations in which I must be ready to obey?

We must return here to the positive alienation spoken of in
Chapter Six. It is true that, in final analysis, I must be my self and
not like the others; yet I start my life in the positive alienation in
which I have to be determined by others and therefore must be
considered to be one like the others. A universal norm corresponds
to such a situation, for such a norm assumes that everyone is like

everyone else. Obedience in this previously described sense, then, is pre-eminently the attitude corresponding to my incipient ethical sensitivity, and my obedient response strengthens this very sensitivity. Let us add that, according as my ethical sensitivity grows, obedience changes its character. When I reach the level where I can personally assume a position with respect to the universal norm, obedience reaches a higher level and becomes a willingness whereby I, involving my ownness, am really ready to *listen* to the normativity of my authentic self and to prevent any arbitrary interpretation of this normativity.

Regarding positive estrangement, one may ask whether it characterizes only the first stage of man's life. Our description may have suggested this idea, which would make positive estrangement a phase to be followed by that of conformism and then rebellion, in order that finally all phases give way to authenticity. Or should it be said that positive alienation is a factor destined to continue to play a role in the entire life-history of man? Let us first point out that positive alienation should not be put on a par with conformism and rebellion, for the simple reason that these two are genuine alienations and therefore ought not to exist; positive estrangement, on the other hand, is needed for self-realization. Let us see why.

Positive alienation is the necessity for man to give up his natural immediacy and acquire a real extension. So we said in Chapter Six, using a formula in line with Hegel. But this formula doesn't show why positive estrangement is needed precisely for man's self-realization. We must therefore add that the ego is in indivisible unity both self-project and project of the world, and this means that the ego is self-project at the same time that it is project of the others. But if I wish to arrive at my own project of the others, I must already have been introduced into the others' domain. This, then, is the positive alienation, which can be described as my thrownness precisely insofar as this term expresses my factical bond with the others. Now, thrownness is invincible because the unfinished condition of the possibilities contained in it can never be definitively completed. Accordingly, conformism and rebellion are phases that can and must be finished, but the positive alienation cannot ultimately be overcome.

A second reflection is needed to clarify the meaning of all this.

The ego is called to his authentic self from the genuine alienation which conformism is. The one who is called, says Heidegger, is the self which understands itself and the world in the way that the impersonal "one" does in everyday existence. In other words, not the one who is with the others in positive alienation is called but the one who has made his home with the others in such a way that he lets himself be determined by them. The call calls the self back from conformism.

To connect these two considerations, the self begins life in positive estrangement, and this estrangement invincibly continues to accompany its life. This means that one starts his life with the presumption that one is a human being like the others. Man cannot avoid starting from this presumption, and it is impossible that this presumption will ever be totally contradicted. Now, the universal norm, which assumes that everyone is like everyone else, is adapted to the inevitable presumption that I am one like the others. For this reason everyone should start with the supposition that the norm valid for all applies also to him. But this presumption can only be maintained as long as no proofs to the contrary present themselves.

The positive estrangement is the thrownness of my being-with-the-others. This thrownness also, which can never totally disappear, must be taken up into the sphere of my project. The ego which doesn't proceed to do this will inevitably pass from the positive alienation to conformism; while there is no longer any need to be determined by the others, he lets himself be determined by them. In such a situation he necessarily hears the call, calling him back from conformism and toward an own project of being-with-the-others. Now, an own project excludes the other's project. The presumption, then, of being like the others is contradicted precisely in one's own project of being-with-the-others. Nevertheless, the necessary presumption continues to hold where it is not contradicted. The self is called to a project of its own, but to an own project of the norm valid for all and therefore to participation in a contemporary interpretation of what is contained in the norm valid for all. It is in this that the proportionate character proper to the authentic self as my norm manifests itself. Accordingly, the proportionate character of the authentic self makes a conformistic following of the universal norm be a genuine alienation.

It is also possible, however, that with respect to a particular human being the presumption of being like the others meets a more radical contradiction. This happens when and insofar as such a man knows that, by wanting to subject himself to the universal norm, he would again be caught in conformism. In other words, it happens insofar as one experiences that a personal interpretation of the universal norm is impossible for him. In such a case the call is heard again, but now as a call to return to himself from his willed harmony with the universal norm which would alienate him from himself in the negative sense of the term.

Such a person can, of course, disregard the call. This would even be much easier than having to come to the painful realization that he is much more radically unlike the others than all those who merely differ in their own interpretation of the universal norm. Nevertheless, he ought to reach the realization that his authentic self doesn't enable him to make a personal interpretation of the norm valid for all. He ought to realize that he must follow his own law in its contradiction to the universal law because otherwise he would disregard the primordial ethical demand of self-realization. It is in this that the appropriateness pertaining to the authentic self as his norm manifests itself.

CHAPTER NINE

God Guarantees
What Is In Principle
Not Transparent

Only the fundamental dimension of religiousness has been discussed until now. In this fundamental sense man is religious when he is not the measure of everything but stands open for reality in its depth and its strangeness, which with respect to him is otherness. The preceding chapter added to this that the ego remains also a stranger to itself because the authentic self presents itself to the ego's freedom as a condition in which it is not at home (*Unheimlichkeit*). That's why man is ethical insofar as he ought to realize his possibilities and why he is religious insofar as he ought to accept his possibilities.

But by what right is being open to otherness called religiousness? We have seen the reasons in Chapter Seven. First of all, this description stands in continuity with an old Christian tradition. Secondly, the description makes sense because one who no longer leaves room for this openness implicitly deifies himself. It is obvious, however, that these considerations are based on the conviction that there is a God or else that a God must be chosen: either there is a God or man is God. This choice also, then, continues to speak in line with a tradition which considers a concept of God meaningful. It thereby simply accepts that the meaningfulness of this tradition can be maintained even today. It is this presupposition that will be discussed in this chapter.

Our starting point will be a problem arising from our preceding considerations. We have defended the ideal of self-realization, but this ideal seems to exclude the possibility of a God. At least, that's the situation presenting itself in Nietzsche, to whom we have appealed when we introduced our ideal.

1. Self-Realization and the Death of God

Let us return to Nietzsche's passage in THUS SPAKE ZARATHUSTRA about the old saint who has fled the company of men. He loved people, too much even, and that was precisely why he fled away from them. Man is "a thing too imperfect" for him, so that love for man would be fatal to him. He now loves God but no longer man. He now praises God. When Zarathustra heard this, he bowed to the saint and parted from him, but in his heart he said: "Could it be possible? This old saint in the forest hath not yet heard of it, that God is dead" (Prologue).

Nietzsche, then, doesn't present the death of God as an isolated event. His death is connected with a certain ethics. One legitimately suspects that Nietzsche opposes himself to a certain ethics which God is supposed to guarantee. What is that connection and what is the ethics in question?

Zarathustra encountered the old saint when he came down from the mountain where he had lived for ten years, gathering wisdom. He encountered him, then, before he revealed to the people the message of his wisdom. The death of God is from the very start an unquestionable presupposition of this message. In this he resembles the young Marx for whom the critique of religion was essentially already finished but who, nonetheless, spoke of it because this critique is the condition of all other critiques. In a similar fashion Nietzsche places the death of God within the perspective of his true interest: "I teach you Superman."

Now, the ethics of the Superman differs from that of man. There is, first of all, an opposition as that between old and new. Old is the saint in the forest; old also was the God who until His last moments was served by an old pope. Nietzsche inscribes new values on new tablets and smashes the old value-tablets of the good and the just. That's why he appears as a criminal in their eyes, but he really is the creative man who establishes something new. He is like a child, innocent and forgetting, and a new start.

This contrast between old and new has three aspects. The old man is contrasted with the Superman, the old Christian morality with a new morality, and the old religion—belief in the survival of the soul, the hereafter and God—with the doctrine that God and the soul are dead. The three old elements are so tightly interconnected that dislodging one means to dislodge the others. Zarathustra mainly tries to undo the old man and his morality, but because of the close interconnection the old God is involved in their downfall.

Who the old man is becomes clear in the last man, the man who wishes to be only man. When he makes his appearance, the earth has become small and on this earth the last man, who makes everything small, hops around. He has withdrawn from the cold countries, for one needs warmth. Sickness and distrust he views as sinful. He takes a little bit of dope from time to time because it gives pleasant dreams, and a lot of it at the end for a pleasant death. People still work, for work relaxes, but they see to it that this relaxation doesn't become too much of an effort. No one desires poverty or wealth; both are too troublesome. Who would still want to obey or to rule? Both are too much bother. The last man says: we have found happiness.

Unsurprisingly, his morality is a morality of little men. He arms himself with all virtues. Few people realize it, of course, but one must have all virtues to get a good night's sleep. Should I covet my neighbor's wife? That would not go together with a good night's sleep. One who has all the virtues still needs to acquire one more, viz., to put all his virtues to sleep at the right moment. Peace with God and peace with one's neighbor—that's demanded for sleeping well.

Just as this morality is a morality of little men, so the God of such people is one who looks after little people. He consoles them in their sorrows. But, most of all, He guarantees their morality. He guarantees it everywhere, even where evil would not come to the surface. For God sees everything, He always sees and His look penetrates into everything. He looks into the depths and the abyss of man, into his hidden shame and ugliness. He penetrates into the dirtiest corners of man with His all-pervading curiosity.

This man, this morality and this God are, in final analysis, connected in one fundamental concept. This, again, reveals itself in the last man who says: "No shepherd and one flock. Everyone wishes the same. Everyone is equal; one who thinks differently goes of his own free will to the asylum." That's why this morality knows no exceptions and is the same for all. That's also the reason why this morality has such a leveling influence and makes man small. And God guarantees that we are all equal: "There are no higher men; we are all equal; man is man, before God we are all equal."

Zarathustra, however, preaches that the time of man is past. Man is something to be overcome. All beings have produced something greater than themselves; would man be the ebb of this great flood? What is the ape for man? An object of laughter and his shame. That's what man ought to be for the Superman. Man is a rope between animal and Superman. What is great about man is that he is a bridge and not a goal, a transition and a passing away. Man is the dark cloud from which the lightning of the Superman must come forth. Superman will be faithful to the earth, for he is the meaning of the earth. "I adjure you, brethren, be faithful to the earth and do not believe those who speak to you of supra-earthly expectations."

Once upon a time the soul looked with disdain upon the body, but that soul itself was thin and emaciated. "On my honor, friend, all that whereof you speak does not exist; there is no devil, no hell. Your soul will die even more quickly than your body; so fear no longer." That's why Zarathustra will entice many away from the herd. He will call them "to follow themselves," not him but themselves. That's why they must first make themselves free to be their own masters in their own desert. Zarathustra will not become angry against one who at night sneaks off to the grave of his God, but his tears are proof of his illness, of a sick body; such a one has not yet become "himself."

"My brother, if you have a virtue and if it is your virtue, you don't have it in common with anyone. Say therefore: 'This is my goodness, this I love, this pleases me, only in this way do I will the good; I do not will it as a law of God, not as a human convention and a necessity; the good is not for me a pointer to a supra-earthly paradise.' " No one knows as yet what good and evil are, except the creative man who gives meaning and a future to the earth and who creatively redeems all that has been. Virtuous is the deed I do now if I know that I would do it over and over again if the opportunity presented itself again. Virtue is obedience to one's own being-as-becoming.

That's why Zarathustra says: "Away with such a God! Rather no God, rather determining one's own destiny with one's own hand, rather a fool, rather being oneself God." This is not impious, Nietzsche thinks. It is precisely Zarathustra's piety, his sensitivity to authentic being which doesn't permit him to believe in a God. "He who gave up God all the more holds fast to belief in morality." Because the event that God is dead is extremely important, our descendants will live in a history that is higher than the old history.[1]

Nietzsche's work THUS SPAKE ZARATHUSTRA undoubtedly shows strongly individualistic and aristocratic features; it preaches ideas which have exercised a nefarious influence but which are no longer held today. The leading thought of his work, however, has become generally accepted. The death of God stands in the perspective of self-realization; the God who is dead is the God who guarantees a Platonic morality of the return in which human ownness and freedom are sacrificed to a law that holds for everyone in the same way. Nietzsche himself admits this explicitly when he says: "Fundamentally only the moral God has been overcome."[2]

This statement says something significant about morality and about God. About morality it says that henceforth morality belongs to the domain in which man has come of age, as Bonhoeffer also observes. Sartre doesn't recognize God's existence, but "even if God did exist, this wouldn't change anything."[3] Even then man would still have to realize himself in creative, inventive freedom. God is no longer the guarantee of the moral order, for man carries the moral ideal in his own bosom, in his authentic self which calls him to his own project of the world and of the others. This authentic

---

[1] Nietzsche, *Thus Spake Zarathustra, passim,* and *Die frohliche Wissenschaft,* nos. 125, 343, 357.

[2] Nietzsche, "Aus dem Nachlass der Achtzigerjahre," *Werke,* Schlechta ed., vol. 3, p. 853.

[3] Sartre, *L'existentialisme est un humanisme,* Paris, 1946, p. 95.

self doesn't need any moral guarantee: man is ethical insofar as the relationship of his project to his authentic self is concerned.

And with respect to God this new situation says that He, if He exists, is not the guarantee of the moral order. We will now proceed to consider whether the authentic self demands a God who guarantees man's fundamental religiousness.

2. The Meaningfulness of Accepting God

The authentic self, we saw, presents itself as a condition of "not being at home" (*Unheimlichkeit*). Even as the text which I have not yet sufficiently interpreted presents itself to me in its invincible otherness, so my own possibilities, insofar as I always haven't yet sufficiently interpreted them, present themselves in their unexpected otherness to my interpreting freedom. Heidegger uses the expression "not being at home" for this situation. He is, of course, not inclined to use this condition as a starting point in a search for religious consequences, but is interested in an analysis of man's being, in this case here an analysis of the call of conscience. On the other hand, he doesn't exclude possible religious consequences.

Yet he wishes to prevent the hasty and therefore premature conclusion that it is God who calls. For the phenomenon of the call belongs to man's own mode of being. He, too, so it seems, is concerned about man's autonomy. Precisely because traditionally the passage to God was made too quickly—a tendency one may wish to ascribe to Platonism—the analysis of man in his own being was neglected, and in consequence of this the realm of human autonomy was made too small. It should be evident that the author of this book wishes to respect Heidegger's attitude in this matter.

Insofar as the authentic self calls man in his freedom to undertake his own self-realization, the calling authentic way of being belongs to the realm of morality. Now morality, as we just saw, belongs to man's autonomy, the realm where man is, in principle, at home with himself.

The statement that morality is a realm in which man has come of age doesn't mean, let us repeat it once more, that morality is a matter of human arbitrariness. If it were, there could be no question of morality, just as there is no morality in the conformistic man. Being-moral implies both norm and freedom. The authentic self is primarily this norm, for it is the only appropriate norm. On the basis of this appropriate norm, I ought to interpret the universal norm in my way—and let us keep in mind that to interpret doesn't mean to read into it something that isn't there. Next, I ought to resist the universal norm wherever I am in a more radical way unlike the others, so that I would become self-estranged by acting as if I were like them. All this we have already said before; it is merely repeated here to give access to a new consideration.

The call of conscience doesn't originate from God. But does this exclude that God can be found by starting from man's authentic self? The rich content of the "condition of not being at home" (*Unheimlichkeit*) offers us an orientation. If the moral man is in principle "at home" with himself, how can his authentic self appear strange to him? How can it constitute a domain in which he is not "at home with himself"? How can man be a stranger with respect to his own unfinished possibilities? Strange as it seems, in the modern thought of not being at home the Platonic idea that man is not at home with himself and in the world returns again. Platonism too quickly and prematurely explained this idea; it disregarded man's bodily condition, fellowman and the world, as if man were in no way at home with them. Thus it disregarded the ego's ownness.

If, however, this idea is stripped of its premature features, so that man's being-of-age can be done justice, it contains also some truth. As was pointed out in the preceding chapter, its truth is at least this that the actually existing reality is not the only reality. In addition, the actual reality is conceivable only on the basis of another reality, viz., the real possibility. But precisely my ego's real possibilities show the characteristic of "not-at-home-ness." And this characteristic is invincible. Hegel wrongly thought that a definitive and total "coming home" is possible. The mature man is the one on whom everything is founded. And man is mature, he has come of age. But his maturity doesn't express his total being because his authentic being continues to present itself to him in unexpected ways, that is, as something that differs from the expectations presumed by anticipating freedom.

This implies, at any rate, that one may ask about the implications of the authentic self. Authentic being is the law calling the ego in its freedom to be itself. Thinking along this line, we discover the moral implications of authentic being. But this discovery doesn't answer the question as to which implications authentic being possesses precisely insofar as it is characterized by strangeness and unexpectedness. Besides, is it right to speak here of implications? Morality, we have said, belongs to the domain where man is at home, with which he is familiar, where he has come of age and enjoys autonomy. Thus not-at-home-ness suggests not only strangeness but also heteronomy. The term "heteronomy," however, is particularly unfortunate; it contains the idea of *nomos*, law, and thus points in the direction of morality. Let's therefore rather say that, even as morality implies independence, so not-at-home-ness suggests the idea of dependence. What is the value of this suggestion?

At the very least this suggestion means that man by his own power can never definitively come to be at home with himself and by his own power he can never be definitively redeemed from the unfinished condition of his possibilities. The expression "by his own power" is used here to indicate that man, although he continues to come more of age all the time, doesn't have the power ever definitively to transcend the strangeness belonging to his own being. With respect to this strangeness man can only assume two attitudes: he either accepts it and rejoices in it or he rejects it and rebels against it, vain as his rebellion may be. This acceptance becomes more difficult according as man more strongly experiences that in his authentic self he is not like the others.

What remains of the above-mentioned suggestion when we stop considering man as such and devote attention to the ego's relationship to the others? The ego cannot redeem itself. Is the reason perhaps because it ought not to be a solitary ego? Isn't the ego pre-eminently redeemed by the others? The authentic man is indeed the ego which brings others to a "plus" of truth; the other is redeemed by me from the unfinished condition of his truth. If this is what love is, then a loving relationship is a mutual redemption. People ought to relate in the fundamental attitude of benevolence— which doesn't mean that they should avoid all conflict. In this way the growth of genuine human relations is a growth in mutual redemption. And because mutual benevolence is based on the recognition of the other man as he is himself—for that's where he is *other*—genuine benevolence and genuine love cannot possibly be based on other motives, such as love for God (if there is a God). The community of man must be a community of love and redemption on its own internal foundation.

Accordingly, the human community, the growing mutual love and reciprocal redemption of human beings also belongs to the domain where man has come of age. This conviction underlies, for example the work of Karl Marx. Nevertheless, this conviction does not weaken the power of the above-mentioned suggestion of dependence. As we pointed out against Marx, strangeness continues to be present in an invincible way even in the human community; hence a definitive final condition in which all strangeness would be transcended cannot be reconciled with man's historicity. We realize that strangeness cannot be thought away from man without removing at the same time man's self-project. For freedom is man's possibility of giving to life a form that doesn't lead away from but leads to his authentic self.

The idea that it belongs to our being-of-age to go forward in creative freedom toward the authentic and non-estranging form of human community presupposes authentic being, and this implies a strangeness which will always continue to contradict our anticipating expectations. Our being-of-age does not take away not-being-at-home. Of necessity we will always be transcended by our own possibilities, but these possibilities belong to our own being. In other words, we are transcended by our own being. Being is our own, it is entrusted to the freedom of our project. But our own being, in the guise of our own possibilities, transcends us. That's why it presents itself to us in not-at-home-ness. It is here that lies the "moment" of our dependence, a dependence, therefore, which is presupposed by our freedom and autonomy. Our autonomy cannot be conceived without this dependence because freedom cannot be conceived without the authentic self.

But, one could say, what else is expressed by the statement that our own possibilities transcend us and that this situation characterizes us in our own being than that man and the community of men are marked with historicity? Nothing else, indeed. However, it is precisely the implication of man's historicity that must be reflected upon. Now, this implication is that our own being transcends us. Isn't this strange? How is it conceivable, how is it possible? The answer is not that man simply happens to be a self-transcending movement. Man is all this, but when one calls man a self-transcending movement, this expression means that man is that movement in which the facticity of his own ego and of the world are transcended toward a new possibility of the ego and the world. This is also the sense in which we have constantly used this expression. The basis on which this self-transcendence is possible is that freedom anticipatingly runs ahead of the authentic self and therefore has always already gone beyond that facticity, has always already transcended it. Here, however, we are not asking how man can transcend facticity, but how our authentic being is possible, how our own possibilities can transcend us, so that we can never definitively realize them.

Shouldn't we very soberly answer that we don't know how this is possible, that it simply *is* so? But what else would such a statement mean but that *in fact* it is so? Such an answer, however, is unsatisfactory. It is unsatisfactory to assign the absolute primacy to facticity, which is what one would do by answering to the question about our possibilities: that's what in fact *is*. Such a primacy of facticity would contradict the essence of man as a being which is already ahead of all facticity because of his orientation to authentic being.

Our question, then, remains meaningful. And the believing affirmation of God is a meaningful answer to this question. That answer is: our authentic being, our own possibilities transcend us because they are offered to us. The offer is not made by our fellowman, for the same question applies also to him. The offer comes from a being of a different order, an order that enables this being to make an offer that greatly transcends the offer of our fellowman. The fellowman is unable to redeem the ego in a definitive way because he also is characterized by historicity, the tension between facticity and authentic being, the not-at-home-ness of authentic being. "Of a different order," then, is only a being which is not characterized by historicity and the above-mentioned tension. This being we call God.

God offers to man man's own possibilities, and His Infinity expresses itself in the invincible, inexhaustible *intensity* of man's own
possibilities. Because it is God who offers man his ownmost possibilities, the latter appear to man as strange, surprising, unexpected,
as the domain where he is not at home with himself. Man's acceptance of his own possibilities is, we said, a deed of fundamental
religiousness. For the man who has reached the recognition of God,
the same acceptance is a deed of religiousness in the full sense of
the term. Religiousness is the recognizing acceptance of my own
existence—with all its limited and, nonetheless, always surprising
possibilities—as an offer made to me by God.

Because God is not characterized by historicity but is the foundation that makes historicity possible, God does not stand at the end
of history as its definitive completion. History doesn't have any
definitive ending point, and God doesn't stand in history, not even
as its ending point. But God makes man and his history possible. He
makes "historizing" mankind an inexhaustible offer which cannot be
definitively completed within our history. But because the tension
between facticity and authentic being doesn't exist in God, He is
identical with His authentic being; that's why He totally realizes
what we call "faithfulness."

God is faithful to His offer. He will therefore maintain his offer
even when man no longer belongs to history. The statement that
God creates man in an offer which cannot be exhausted in history
because man is unable to redeem himself definitively from the
incompleteness of his possibilities means that God creates man for
immortality. Standing in history, man must hermeneutically use his
time of life to attain self-realization. God's faithfulness to His offer
means that He will use immortality for this man in order to redeem
him from his incompleteness in a way that will excede all expectations—to infinity.[4]

Finally, this God doesn't present Himself as the guarantee of the
moral order but rather as the guarantee of my authentic self and
that of all mankind. For our own possibilities, unfinished but de-

---

[4] Cf. William A. Luijpen, " 'De erwtensoep is klaar', een filosofische be-
schouwing over de geloofsakt," *Streven*, XXII (1969), deel II, no. 5, pp.
510-526.

manding completion, are offered to us by a God who will be faithful to His offer. God guarantees something that is still strange to us, viz., that which we have presumed by anticipation but which precisely for this reason continues to retain a margin of invincible opaqueness.

3. *God Is Not the Guarantee of "Clear and Distinct Ideas"*

The thoughts formulated above show the distance separating us from the Greek and Cartesian ideal. In Chapter One we have discussed the Greek ideal of *theoria,* contemplation; let us now, to finish this book, illustrate the distance we have travelled by considering and criticizing Descartes' concept of God.

At the start of his philosophy Descartes enumerates the reasons he has to doubt all accepted truths. He adds force to these reasons by having recourse to an extreme hypothesis. Let us assume, he says, that there exists an "evil genius, cunning and powerful, who bends every effort to deceive me. But even then there is an "Archimedian point," even if he deceives me, *I am,* I am as a thinking being, for to doubt and to be deceived is to think. But in everything else that genius could deceive me. Why am I so certain that I am? Because I understand it clearly and distinctly. In this way I am inclined to accept as true everything which I clearly and distinctly understand. This inclination, however, could perhaps be the effect of the influence exercised on me by that great deceiver. That's why I must first ask myself on whom I am dependent—on that deceiving genius or on a God; and if I know that there is a God, I must ask myself whether God can deceive me. "For if I don't establish the truth about these two points, I don't see how I can ever be certain about anything."[5]

After ascertaining his own existence, then, Descartes must prove that there is a God. He employs the following consideration. Mathematicians prove that the angles of a triangle are equal to two right angles. Now, if I consider the concept "perfect being" which I have in myself, I see that this concept implies existence, just as the concept "triangle" implies that its angles are equal to two right

---

[5] *Méditations métaphysiques,* 3rd. medit.

angles. "Accordingly, that God, this perfect being, exists is at least just as certain as a mathematical proof is certain."[6]

God's existence helps me in the question about truth. For everything which my mind could clearly and distinctly think, everything which could contain truth and perfection, is already contained in the idea "all-perfect God." God, then, cannot deceive me. The inclination I have to ascribe truth to clear and distinct ideas cannot be the result of deception. God has given me the power to judge. He could, of course, have created me in such a way that I would have clear and distinct ideas about everything, so that I would never be subject to mistakes. But I shouldn't complain that I don't belong to the most noble and perfect category. For if I limit myself to judging only matters into which I have a clear and distinct insight, I cannot be mistaken.

Certainty about God's existence has still another consequence. I am unable to keep my attention always focussed on a single point; that's why I don't continue to contemplate the reasons which made me accept a certain thing and why then sometimes other reasons present themselves to me "which would make me change my view if I didn't know that there is a God. Thus I would never be able to possess a true and certain knowledge about anything."[7] After demonstrating that the angles of a triangle are equal to two right angles, I could proceed to another consideration and then I could easily begin to doubt that demonstrated truth if I didn't know that there is a God. For I could then think that my nature is such that I can easily make a mistake. No science would then be possible. However, after recognizing that there is a God who doesn't deceive and understanding that every clear and distinct insight is true, I need no longer think about the arguments; I merely need to remember that I clearly and distinctly understood the matter.

"In this way," says Descartes, "I clearly see that the certainty and truth of every science depend on the knowledge of the true God, so that, prior to knowing Him, I am unable to have any perfect knowledge. And now that I know Him, I am able to acquire a perfect science about many things, not only about matters that are in Him, but also about things pertaining to bodily nature insofar as

---

[6] Descartes, *Discours de la méthode,* Ch. 4.
[7] *Méditations métaphysiques,* at the end of the 5th medit.

this nature is the object of the proofs of mathematicians, who themselves do not pay attention to His existence."[8]

Descartes' God is the victory over the hypothesis of a deceiving God; from the very start He is involved in the question whether man can attain the truth. Descartes presents God as the guarantor of the truth and man's desire for truth. But a true statement requires clear and distinct ideas, the prototype of which is constituted by mathematical ideas. That's why God guarantees science and man's desire for science. God's existence, then, is not just "at least as certain" as a mathematical demonstration; it is most certain, for the certainty of mathematics is based on the certainty that God exists.

Descartes' man is clearly characterized by a natural desire for science and mathematics. That's why it is so unfortunate that man also has confused ideas. These ideas he didn't get from God; as God's creature, man only has clear and distinct insights. His confused ideas are not guaranteed by God. Man has confused ideas insofar as he participates in nothingness, for "I am, as it were, midway between God and nothingness."[9] Confused ideas, therefore, are without any guarantee and will seduce man to untrue judgments. God could have made man in such a way that he would have had only clear and distinct ideas, but as a matter of fact He hasn't done so. Why He failed to do this is a matter which Descartes cannot answer.

The parallelism between Descartes' God and Descartes' man is very striking. Both are very interested in science. Or are both primarily interested in the truth? But Descartes narrows the range of truth to truth which either is axiomatic or can be deduced from axioms through a stringent demonstration, in other words, the truth of mathematics. Such a God is not interested in the everyday life of the ordinary man—no more than is the mathematician when he pursues his science. The idea that truth can have something to do with life cannot arise here. God isn't interested in the history of mankind—no more than history forms part of the object of mathematics. In such a perspective the idea that history itself could be the coming to be of truth would be unintelligible.

---

[8] *Ibid.*

[9] Descartes, *op. cit.*, 4th medit.

Such a parallelism between God and man must be based on an anthropomorphism, for science is a typically human possibility. This means that Descartes conceived God *in terms of* a typically human possibility. Such an idea of God could, of course, not be maintained when man acquired a more refined understanding of his own functions. This point became evident when Husserl took up again Descartes' meditations. Husserl also is interested in the foundation of science, but after so many centuries it has become evident, he says, where Descartes failed. Let us posit, Husserl argues, that with Descartes I try to "bracket" all accepted certainties, including those about the world, and subject them to methodic doubt. I'll then experience that such an attempt fails. It must fail of necessity, in the sense that the world which I wanted to leave out didn't really disappear from me. It continues to present itself. As phenomenon, the world cannot be denied. For no leaving out of the world can effect that our experience is no longer an experience of the world. That's why the world must be the chief theme of phenomenological description.

But how is this possible? Hasn't Descartes shown that our knowledge sometimes deceives us and therefore can also deceive us now? And doesn't this make every attempt to describe the world suspect? Mustn't we renounce the world and investigate our own ideas, as Descartes did? The answer is in the negative; we cannot renounce the world. And it *is* possible to describe the world. There is, of course, reason for uncertainty, but doubt and uncertainty are limited and must be kept within their limits. They never affect the world in its totality. At most we can suspect that here or there the world differs from what I thought and that I have to remove certain things from it as "mere appearance," "hallucination," "dream," etc. Moreover, the description of the world will never manage to discover everything at once. We will gradually learn that a distinction must be made between more or less restricted and fundamental experiences. This distinction will present itself spontaneously to us; we don't need any constructs or mathematical proofs of it. "The 'life-world' is a realm of original experiences," says Husserl, and that which is evident presents itself.[10]

---

[10] Husserl, "Die irrige Auffassung einer abgekapselten Seel," Beilage VII of *Phänomenologische Psychologie*, The Hague, 1962, pp. 385-389; *Pariser Vorträge*, The Hague, 1950 (p. 8: "Alles bleibt wie es war.").

Accordingly, Husserl doesn't accept the hypothesis of a "deceiving God" and he rejects therefore the idea which makes God the Victory over such a hypothesis. Independently of God truth can be discovered and a foundation given to science. The God who functions in the service of a typically human possibility is unseated as such now that it becomes evident that man can exercise his own function independently.

Husserl's ideas in this matter are taken up again by Merleau-Ponty, particularly in the Preface to his PHENOMENOLOGY OF PERCEPTION. But Merleau-Ponty also connects there the Cartesian ideal of clarity with the Greek ideal of *theoria*. Let us see how.

I am always involved in the world. But if with Descartes I would withdraw to my own ideas and ask myself whether I am dreaming or awake, I would already have disregarded the world. For the fact that I am able to ask whether I am dreaming and imagining things proves that I have experience of reality on the one hand and of dreaming and imagining on the other. I must therefore analyze these experiences. And the fact that we make a distinction between evidence and illusion shows that we already know what an illusion is. We know this because we have already had an evident contact with the world.

Accordingly, the fact that we are able to doubt discloses our power to unmask untruth. We cannot be totally torn away from truth; we are in the realm of truth and it is the experience of truth which is self-evident. But we shouldn't look for absolute evidence; we shouldn't try to base the evidence of the world on an absolute clarity of our thoughts. For we would then become unfaithful to our experience of the world. If there were absolute clarity, I'd possess the world. But I don't possess it, for the world is inexhaustible.

Man is a project of the world, orientated to a world which he doesn't encompass and cannot possess but to which he doesn't cease to orientate himself. Because the world is unceasingly the end intended by the human project, man doesn't orientate himself only now and then to the world; for instance, when he makes a judgment and arrives at a decision. Such actions originate only within a unity of ourselves and the world that is always already present, in other words, within the project. That's why there is a clear distinction between "comprehension" and "intellection." "Intellection" is limited to "true and immutable essences," but "comprehension" can grasp their *genesis*, the history of their origin. "Intellection" concludes that truth is pre-given and precedes our knowledge, but "comprehension" sees that truth comes about only in our project. Truth comes about through our initiative "which has no guarantee in being."[11]

Merleau-Ponty's reflections show that the God of Greek *theoria* strongly resembles the God of Descartes. The God of *theoria* is the bearer of the essences; the truth lies in these and man merely has to discover this truth. Because the essences are fixed and immutable and give rise to clear and distinct conceptual knowledge, God guarantees both the essences and the truth. The empirical dimension or at least the individual dimension—the individual freedom and the history of the particular human being and of mankind in general—remain irretrievably confused and ambiguous because they escape conceptual knowledge. They are therefore not guaranteed in any way, they don't lead to truth and may not be appealed to. They are suspected of arbitrariness, wilfullness and ethical unreliability. The same verdict applies to the written word because it continues to offer resistance to any attempt to give it a definitive interpretation. Its value with respect to truth is less than that of the spoken word. For only the spoken word is almost totally one with the thought, which ought to be clear and distinct.

Such a way of looking at things fails to do justice to historicity. For historicity gives expression to the unity of the various parts of time; the unfinished past depends on the interpreter who can only live now insofar as, in a presumptive anticipation, he projects a completion of the past forward toward the future. The thinking of *theoria* knows only the past. But such a thinking disregards historicity because it wrongly conceives the past as finished and tacitly assumes that the passage of time is a loss that must be stopped and undone, that time exposes me to the danger of losing the essential truth which I already possess.

But the God who is the guarantor of truth which has been established once and for all is dead. He could not maintain Himself when man discovered that he is free, an original initiative, an

---

11 *Phénoménologie de la Perception*, Preface, esp. pp. XI, XIII and XV.

irrevocable ownness, an autonomous being, responsible for tasks that are his own and which can no longer be shifted to God. It must be admitted, of course, that as early as the Middle Ages Thomas Aquinas pointed out that whoever does an injustice to man's dignity fails to do justice to God;[12] nevertheless, it is only in our time that the range of man's autonomy has become evident. Man must extend his control over the entire range of the world; God must be "expelled" from that domain.

Nevertheless, the affirmation of God remains possible and meaningful and doesn't contradict man's self-realization. It remains possible because man is not the master of history nor the measure of everything. On the contrary, man is measured by the invincible intensity of all that is. The affirmation of God remains meaningful because it is a meaningful answer to the not-at-home-ness, the strangeness which characterizes all beings in their intensity and which man himself also always continues to reveal to himself. And it doesn't contradict man as a self-realizing being because not-at-home-ness is a condition of freedom and autonomy.

This God, however, can no longer be appealed to to guarantee functions which man himself must fulfill. Our considerations have shown that one puts obstacles in the way of the development of future religiousness if one continues to see God as the guarantor of established truth and unambiguous certainties. We are not pleading here for deliberate ambiguity; man's thinking must strive for greater clarity, for otherwise it would no longer be thinking. But we are arguing against the kind of hasty clarity, gained at the cost of individuality and history, a clarity which is born from an impoverishment and then subjects people to an impoverished reality in which they can no longer recognize themselves.

The fact that Nietzsche in his resistance to accepted morality proclaimed the death of God and the fact that Husserl re-assigned the whole of reality to philosophy are not isolated events. The process of secularization also is concerned with liberating reality from its impoverishment. There are authors who say that secularization is a struggle against the Christian concept of reality. It must

---

12 *Contra gentes*, bk. 3, ch. 68: "Detrahere ergo perfectioni creaturarum est detrahere perfectioni divinae virtutis"; and *ibid.*, ch. 78; "Exigit igitur divinae providentiae ratio ut ceterae creaturae per creaturas rationales regantur."

indeed be admitted that Christianity identified itself with Platonism; this, however, was a premature position, one, therefore, that can be discarded and then leaves open the possibility of a Christian concept of reality which doesn't unduly narrow or impoverish reality. Nevertheless, such a narrowing view will of necessity occur again, albeit in a modified form, because by rejecting Platonism *in toto* one casts out not only its untruth but also its element of truth. This truth, we think, is that actually existing reality is not the only kind of reality; reality consists of the components of actuality and possibility; and the primacy belongs to possible reality rather than actual reality. This is a point that could be brought to bear against the reductive hermeneutics of Paul Van Buren.

If this is so, then *the full breadth* of actual reality is worthy of man's attention, and at the same time is also transcended in the direction of its inexhaustible wealth of possibilities. Man's proper task is to realize these possibilities. He is able to do this, despite the fact that the future doesn't yet have any content, because the possibilities in question are possibilities arising from the past. This past cannot give him any rules with a fixed content; nevertheless, it functions as a norm which receives a content from man's interpretation, and presently it will induce him again to make a new interpretation, which again will be governed by the same norm although it doesn't have the same content. God doesn't enter into this human task, but it is God who offers man his task.

For man's self-realization it need not make any difference whether or not he knows that God makes him this offer. But one who knows could go forward to the infinity of the future with greater confidence. The future is uncertain and the possibilities of failure are numberless. God will not interfere when man's own efforts fail, but neither will He withdraw His infinite offer because of man's failure. And even where man doesn't fail there remains an invincible distance between what he has accomplished and what presents itself for accomplishment. One who knows of God realizes that precisely in this invincible distance God remains faithful to His offer. He realizes that God will surpass mankind's expectations—to infinity.

INDEX OF NAMES

INDEX OF SUBJECT MATTER